VGM Opportunities Series

OPPORTUNITIES IN
TRAINING & DEVELOPMENT CAREERS

Edward E. Gordon
Catherine M. Petrini
Ann P. Campagna

Foreword by
Anthony Carnevale
Vice President, Public Leadership
Educational Testing Service

658.3124
G662

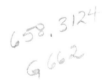

VGM Career Horizons
a division of *NTC Publishing Group*
Lincolnwood, Illinois USA

DEDICATION

To all future workforce education managers
who wish to better support the learning organization
throughout American business.

Cover Photo Credits
Upper left courtesy of Roland/Diamond Associates, Inc., 67 Emerald
Street, Keene, New Hampshire; upper right courtesy of IBM; lower right
courtesy of Mazda; lower left courtesy of the American Society for
Training and Development.

Library of Congress Cataloging-in-Publication Data

Gordon, Edward E.
  Opportunities in training and development careers / Edward E.
Gordon, Catherine M. Petrini, Ann P. Campagna.
    p.   cm. — (VGM opportunities series)
  Includes bibliographical references (p.).
    ISBN 0-8442-4643-3 (alk. paper). — ISBN 0-8442-4644-1 (pbk. :
alk. paper)
    1. Employees—Training of—Vocational guidance.   2. Career
development—Vocational guidance.   I. Petrini, Catherine M.
II. Campagna, Ann P.   III. Title.   IV. Series.
HF5549.5.T7G5368   1997
331.25'92'023—dc20   96-27794
                                                              CIP

Published by VGM Career Horizons, a division of NTC Publishing Group
4255 West Touhy Avenue
Lincolnwood (Chicago), Illinois 60646-1975, U.S.A.
© 1997 by NTC Publishing Group. All rights reserved.
No part of this book may be reproduced, stored in a retrieval
system, or transmitted in any form or by any means,
electronic, mechanical, photocopying, recording or otherwise,
without the prior permission of NTC Publishing Group.
Manufactured in the United States of America.
6 7 8 9 VP 9 7 6 5 4 3 2 1

CONTENTS

The knowledge revolution. The evolution of training. The future of education at work.

What trainers do. Training program design/development. Identifying needs. Developing program objectives. Program content. Training methods. Program evaluation. Training program implementation. Train-the-trainer workshops. Presentation skills. The training leader. The facilitator as change agent.

Compensation. Working conditions. Personal motivations.

Sweeping changes. Training institutes. Training package certification programs. Competency model. College training and development programs. New credentials for the corporate university.

LIST OF FIGURES

ABOUT THE AUTHORS

Edward E. Gordon has established himself as an internationally known authority on employee training and education in the workplace through his publications and speeches. He is the principal author of *FutureWork, the Revolution Reshaping American Business* (Praeger, 1991), *Closing the Literacy Gap in American Business* (Greenwood, 1991), *Ethics for Training and Development* (ASTD, 1995), and *Workforce Education: Improving Educational Skills* (ASTD, 1993). Gordon has authored numerous articles on innovative training and development practices in *Training & Development* (ASTD), *Performance and Instruction* (NSPI), *Workforce* (ICESA), and *Workforce Training News/Corporate University Review* as well as other publications.

A frequent keynote speaker on current issues in education and training, Gordon has addressed such groups as The Conference Board, the National Conference of State Directors of Adult Education and GED Administrators, the Railroad Personnel Association, American Management Association (AMA), and the American Society for Training and Development (ASTD).

Gordon is president of Imperial Corporate Training & Development, a Chicago-based management consulting firm. He serves on the boards of the Private Industry Council of Cook County, the National Council for Business-Education Cooperation, the Illinois Literacy Resources Development Center, the Illinois Business-Education Partnership Board, and the Better Business Bureau of Chicago and Northern Illinois.

Gordon holds a doctorate in psychology and the history of education from Loyola University of Chicago. He has taught at DePaul and Roosevelt Universities and is currently an instructor at Loyola University of Chicago in the Adult Corporate Instructional Management Program. He is the author of *Centuries of Tutoring: A History of Alternative Education in America and Western Europe* (University Press of America, 1990), *Educator's Consumer Guide to Private Tutoring Services* (Phi Delta Kappa, 1989), and a number of articles in educational journals about contemporary issues and practices in tutoring.

Catherine M. Petrini, a novelist and nonfiction writer and editor, is the former managing editor of *Training & Development* magazine, the flagship publication of the American Society for Training and Development. In her seven years at *T&D,* she worked to improve the quality of writing and editing on the magazine and led efforts to develop ASTD's editorial stylebook. She helped oversee three *T&D* redesigns, a conversion to electronic pagination, and a name change. Through her work at ASTD, she has gained extensive contacts and knowledge in the field of training and development.

Now a full-time novelist, Petrini escapes reality by writing pseudonymous books for teenagers. She has more than a dozen young-adult novels to her credit, all written for popular teen series. They include action-adventure thrillers, romances, mysteries, and a book about a werewolf terrorizing London.

Petrini is active in the field of communications. She is secretary of the National Federation of Press Women and past-president of the Washington, DC, NFPW affiliate, Capital Press Women. She is also a member of Washington Independent Writers, the Society of Children's Book Writers and Illustrators, Washington Edpress, and the National Women's Book Association. Her articles have appeared in various national newsletters and magazines for writers and editors. She also has spoken to groups around the country on writing-related topics ranging from "How to Get Published in HRD" to "How to Write for Children." She has won awards for her fiction and nonfiction work from the National Federation of Press Women, Capital Press Women, the Washington Society, and the American Society of Association Executives.

Petrini lives in Alexandria, Virginia, and holds a degree from the University of Virginia.

Ann P. Campagna has spent her entire career in the field of education and training. Her background includes school administration, director of education programs at a large city hospital, and manager of training at a *Fortune* 500 company. Today she divides her time between managing training programs and projects at Imperial Corporate Training and Development and working as an associate with Doherty International and Options Unlimited. Campagna also conducts workshops and seminars for all levels of learners, elementary school through adult.

A graduate of Rosary College, River Forest, Illinois, she also holds a master's of science degree from Marquette University. Campagna serves as a member of the Board of Directors of STEPS, a Milwaukee-based organization educating adults in the workplace.

ACKNOWLEDGMENTS

The authors wish to acknowledge the important contributions of the following individuals who provided them with career information for this book: Angela Durante, National-Louis University; Julie Furst-Bowd, University of Wisconsin, Stout; Linda Jeleniewski, Illinois Institute of Technology; Ronald Morgan, Loyola University, Chicago; Judith Ponticell, Texas Tech University; Michael Stelnicki, Governors State University; and Joy Thompson, College of St. Francis. Gratitude is also due to Linda Kanter, who contributed data from her master's thesis research at De Paul University, Chicago, and to the staff at the ASTD Information Center, who helped to compile the bibliography.

We also wish to thank the many individuals who contributed their ideas for this book, including Elaine H. Gordon, for her expert editing, research, and criticism, which greatly improved the final product. We also wish to thank Sandra Gula Gleason, who prepared the final manuscript for publication. This book owes its accuracy and graphics to her superb computer abilities. The authors take sole responsibility for whatever errors or shortcomings the reader finds in the text.

FOREWORD

We are all trainers. We all spend time advising and instructing others—including family members, co-workers, and the occasional stranger in need of assistance. Some of us find a particular joy in empowering or enabling others. These are the people who make the best trainers. Their primary qualification for the training craft is a generosity of spirit that makes them want to share the power and delight inherent in knowing, rather than limit access to know-how in order to control or exclude others.

Currently, more than half of us need training to qualify for our jobs, and more than 40 percent of working Americans are retrained after they are on the job.

As *Opportunities in Training and Development Careers* demonstrates, we will need more trainers and teachers in the future to help us adapt to a more dynamic culture and economy. Skill requirements are going up in every occupation and industry. As skill requirements increase, more of us will need training to qualify for our jobs and training to keep up with skill changes on the job. Job opportunities are already extensive for trainers and will grow in the future.

Training will be even more necessary to help us cope with change. The pace of economic and cultural change is accelerating as new transportation, communication, and information technologies increase human interaction in the diverse global community. In the modern work place, machines and computers are taking on more and more of the rote physical and mental labor, leaving workers to interact with each other and with customers to make the best use of the new technology and to provide greater quality and convenience. In a work environment where the volume of human interaction is increasing, we will need to be trained in interpersonal, communication and other interactive skills in order to add value to products and services.

In addition, we will need better education and more training to help us respond to the growing diversity in the American work place. As human interaction increases on the job, our diverse workforce can either create conflict in the work place or result in the creativity inherent in diverse perspectives.

New learning requirements also have expanded throughout the life cycle. The days when all of us moved in lockstep from school to work and into retirement are passing. As change accelerates, learning has become a lifelong activity. As learning becomes more continuous and pervasive, the focus of learning has also moved beyond the traditional boundaries of the classroom into families, communities, and workplaces, blurring the distinction between education and training. New information technologies promise the final dissolution of institutional barriers to learning and the gradual emergence of a global and virtual classroom in which individuals tailor learning to their own needs and interests.

In the virtual classroom, trainees will learn at their own pace; trainers will need to do less teaching. Instead, in a virtual world, the trainer will need to master new communications and other information-based technologies to make them a transparent medium for delivering learning directly to students. In a more flexible and technology-based learning environment, the trainers will be more like learning coaches, enabling trainees to develop their own abilities to access knowledge and learn.

Anthony Carnevale
Vice President, Public
Leadership
Educational Testing Service

PREFACE

Over the past twenty-eight years people have approached me many times for information on how to get into the training and development profession. As a past officer of the Chicagoland Chapter of the American Society for Training and Development (CCASTD), I saw thousands of adults attending monthly chapter meetings looking for an organized professional development program that would give them the big picture of what a career in training and development is all about. They also sought to find personal educational growth opportunities that would enable them to successfully enter the profession of adult workplace educator.

I discovered that there was a general lack of career and educational information on the training and development field readily available for students and adults. The idea behind this book is to help fill in this career knowledge void with accurate and understandable information.

Given our various backgrounds, my co-authors and I are able to present three perspectives to the reader regarding workplace education: that of a training manager/consultant, an association publication manager/writer, and a consulting firm executive/university instructor. We have combined our different viewpoints to give you what we hope is a balanced, collaborative overview.

The role of lifelong learning in every business both large or small continues to assume greater strategic importance. However, if this trend is to continue and successfully establish education as a "profit driver" throughout America, we must better prepare the

next generation of professional trainers. Adult workforce education is a distinct profession demanding careful educational preparation and continuous professional development. We know more
today about how to teach adults at work successfully than ever
before. Adult workforce educators are also managers in a business
environment. Preparing them as business managers is a prerequi-
site if training and development ever hopes to gain acceptance as
an important strategic operating factor in business.

Edward E. Gordon
Catherine Petrini
Ann Campagna

CHAPTER 1

THE EVOLUTION OF WORKPLACE TRAINING & DEVELOPMENT

THE KNOWLEDGE REVOLUTION

Never before in world history has increasing personal knowledge assumed such importance for most members of the workforce. Why? Because even as you read this, rapid technological changes are making more jobs obsolete.

In 1970, the personal computer (PC) did not exist. By 1995, 100 million PCs were in use worldwide. The rise of quality, teams, empowerment, critical thinking, and an endless list of new training perspectives is being relentlessly pushed forward. As old occupations fade, new jobs are being created by this all-pervasive technological revolution.

Brains over brawn means that lifelong education is here to stay for U.S. workers. Many of them will experience job obsolescence throughout their careers no matter what occupation they choose. How U.S. business and educational institutions address this phenomenon will be a critical factor in determining whether the year 2000 and beyond will also be another "American century."

How will future trainers and educators of adults in the workplace address this great challenge? To begin finding answers to this question, it is helpful to review how training and development evolved in the United States and is now shaping the future of work-force education.

THE EVOLUTION OF TRAINING

Early Craft Training—European Origins (Before 1820)

Early America did not invent the concept of specific training for each individual craft or trade. In ancient Sumeria, Egypt, Greece, and Rome the astounding architectural and masonry works of craftspeople were embodied in their pyramids, temples, forums, aqueducts, and amphitheaters.

Because literacy was limited, the skills and knowledge of stone-masons, brick masons, and carpenters were transmitted mainly through direct instruction. However, from surviving records we know that scribes (writers) and priests were trained in temple schools that used written instruction.

During the European high Middle Ages (twelfth to fifteenth centuries) craft, trade, merchant, and university professor guilds established specific training experiences. This helped ensure that individual work met established standards of quality. The great cathedrals of medieval Europe stand as a dramatic testimony to the success of this early training system. Over a period of only several hundred years (1100–1350), the majority of these enormous buildings were constructed by these craftspeople using the most primitive tools and machinery.

The early universities of Europe (Paris, Oxford, Cambridge, Bologna, Florence) also trained teachers through a specific apprenticeship program. Each guild (arts, medicine, law, philosophy) established the criteria for specific levels of scholarship. The B.A., M.A., and Ph.D. signified a license to teach as a "master" or a "doctor" as detailed by the regulations established by each discipline's guild. These were the early origins of the modern university.

Colonial America adapted this apprenticeship system from Europe. This guild system was a precursor of the modern union movement. It carefully regulated members' conditions, tools, wages, and, most importantly, the training process of each student.

At the top of this work hierarchy was the fully trained master. He had many years of experience. Through the local guild, he enforced professional craft quality standards and regulated the training of new workers. He supplied the tools and materials and managed his shop. Apprentices, who lived with the master, learned their trade by passing through prescribed stages of training. If successful, they became journeymen traveling from town to town, receiving a fixed wage for their labors. Some remained in their master's shop to gain the requisite knowledge and take their final craft examination. If the journeyman passed the guild's examination, he became a master craftsman and was entitled to set up his own shop. Modern Germany continues to use a formal craft training program as part of its "dual educational system."

The apprenticeship system never worked well in early America because of a severe shortage of skilled labor. Colonial America was largely an agrarian economy based on small farms. There were few large cities. Most manufactured goods were imported from Europe. As a result the majority of potential workers were never employed as tradesmen but were either farmers or associated with the shipping trade.

The characteristics of the master-apprentice-journeyman craft system made it a very close-knit work team (see Figure 1.1). Apprentices were often viewed by masters as sons. Though the technologies employed were meager and simple, this working-by-doing learning approach required a very long-term commitment. The training program was geared to the individual artisan's craft needs and expectations. Employee motivation was critical to the success or failure of the entire training system.

The Industrial Revolution (1820–1914)

By 1820 the Industrial Revolution was well under way in America. An average of seventy-seven patents was issued each year prior to 1810. By 1860 Yankee ingenuity had raised the annual average to more than 4,500.

Industrialization required training for specific tasks. The pattern of stable, lifelong occupations began to change. Work was not home-based but became focused on larger, depersonalized organizations that were usually established in growing urban areas.

Between 1820 and the outbreak of World War I (1914), factory schools were established to supplant the apprenticeship system. Hoe and Company, a manufacturer of printing presses founded in 1872, established one of the first factory schools to train machinists. As the nineteenth century advanced, available machinists often proved incapable of operating more complex technology. Until that time most machinists had relied on rule-of-thumb methods and had neither the mathematical nor the technical knowledge required to make precision parts.

Factory schools were established by Westinghouse (1888), General Electric (1901), International Harvester (1907), Western Electric (then part of AT&T), Ford, National Cash Register, and many other manufacturers. They provided specific task education within the emerging modern business organization.

This early industrial period was driven by a workforce of largely unskilled machine operators (see Figure 1.1). Both unskilled and skilled workers were viewed as a variable cost. Worker employment fluctuated with market demands. The overall educational opportunities available to most Americans were extremely limited. Private schools were dominant until the end of the nineteenth century.

Figure 1.1. Evolution of Training and Development in America

	Early Craft Training (Before 1820)	Industrial Revolution (1820–1914)	Mass Production Era (1915–1945)	Cold War Era (1946–1992)	Workforce 2000 (1992–2000)
Workforce	Master, journeyman, apprentice	Unskilled machine operators	Interchangeable division of unskilled labor driven by machine pacing	Groups of workers under a supervisor	Self-directed work teams
View of Workers	Apprentices often seen as sons	Unskilled and skilled workers considered a variable cost	Workers may be substituted anywhere on the assembly line	Workers long-term, career-oriented community members	A human resource that needs constant development
Employment Time Frame	Long-term	Determined by market fluctuations	Some market fluctuations, seniority governs layoffs	Employment stability	Very changeable, intermittent
Technology	Meager and simple	New machines evolve with new energy sources	Machines dominate	Complex technology	Rapidly changing, interactive, high-tech
Training and Development Offered	Organized for individual employee needs	Less skills training for fewer people	Functional expertise and administrative efficiency expertise	Team building, technical skills, retraining	Lifelong learning that responds to change
Employee Motivation	Very important to craft system	Decreasing need	Decreasing need	Promotion, raises, benefits	Vested in job changes and job enrichment

The Production Era (1915–1945)

In 1910 Henry Ford introduced assembly line manufacturing based on Frederick Taylor's principles of scientific management. The assembly line system consisted of small divisions of labor and machine work, thus reducing the need for skilled workers. An individual tightened a specific bolt rather than assembling a complete product. Workers were not required to think, learn, adapt, or solve problems—only to endlessly perform mechanically simple tasks.

World War I (1914–1918) provided a major stimulus for mass production. Charles R. Allen's "four-step method" (show, tell, do, and check) became a standard method for on-the-job training (OJT) adopted by burgeoning assembly line war industries.

Between 1890 and 1920 the United States moved from a rural, agrarian-based economy to an urban, industrialized society. By 1918 all forty-eight states had enacted mandatory tax-supported school attendance for all children. Why?

A new relationship existed between the social and economic forces spawned by the U.S. Industrial Revolution. Schooling was found to be one of the best ways of inculcating such productive worker values as punctuality, respect for authority, quality work, and self-discipline. These were the essential work-ethic demands of the new twentieth-century, mass-production, urban society.

The tax-supported public school emerged through alliances of business, union, political, educational, and social reform associations. These diverse groups agreed that the American workplace needed people trained with greater general knowledge (literacy) and better technical skills (vocational education). The public schools would provide the functional context for teaching the elements of the mechanical arts and natural sciences needed for lifelong employment.

The ending of the Great Depression, with America's entry into World War II (1941–1945), sparked a reformulation of the OJT approach. America became the "arsenal of democracy" during World War II, defeating the Axis powers (Germany, Japan, Italy) with mountains of assembly line products. These tanks, guns, trucks, and jeeps all had mass-produced, interchangeable parts made by many different manufacturers, all of whom used assembly line training systems.

A train-the-trainer system called Job Instructor Training (JIT) was designed for first-line and second-line supervisors to support the expansion of assembly line production in the U.S. defense industry. More than 2 million supervisors received JIT or offshoot programs in job methods and human relations.

During the mass-production era (1915–1945) the workforce was composed of large numbers of unskilled men (and, for the first time, women), who were largely interchangeable and driven by machine pacing (see Figure 1.1). Employment downturns occurred at the end of World War I and during the Great Depression. Layoffs were based on seniority. A machine technology clearly dominated. The training provided by business stressed functional expertise and administrative efficiency. Individual employee motivation was not considered an important factor in making this system successful.

The Cold War Era (1946–1992)

The United States emerged from World War II as the most powerful and prosperous nation on earth—a position it enjoyed until the 1990s. The technologies that had made America a world power were now exported overseas. A postwar baby boom helped ensure that the great industrial capacity built during the war years was retooled to support a large-scale, consumer-driven society. Management development was mobilized to meet these new complexities of production and distribution by using the military chain-of-command model, which included twelve layers of management.

By the early 1950s business training began to focus on supervisory development. This interest was directed, at least in part, by the rediscovery of Elton Mayo's Hawthorne studies, conducted in the late 1920s and early 1930s at the Hawthorne plant of Western Electric, near Chicago. This was the telephone manufacturing arm of AT&T, which then employed more than 40,000 workers. The Hawthorne studies led to the recognition that managers trained in leadership can influence human relations, thereby improving employee morale and personal motivation.

Later studies debated whether this "Hawthorne effect" was behind the achievement of desirable productivity goals. Additional research conducted during the 1950s by James Worthy, Charles Walker, and Robert Guest documented the negative effects of repetitive, low-skilled, machine-paced work on employee morale and productivity.

For the first time in American history, the Engineering, Science and Management War Training program (ESMWT), established during World War II, and the GI Bill after the war, exposed millions of adults to college courses on almost every aspect of management, technology, psychology, and education. These continuing education and management training programs provided the impetus to the formation of the American Society for Training and Development (1944) and fueled the vast expansion of the American Management Association (founded in 1923). These organizations helped increase the popularity of off-site management and executive development programs. By the mid-1950s human resource development (HRD) had become a widely respected field. Training and development clearly emerged as a vital part of overall human resources (see Figure 1.2). Training and development programs began to feature business games, "in-basket" exercises, simulations, and the extensive use of role-playing exercises.

Figure 1.2.   Human Resource Wheel

TRAINING & DEVELOPMENT
focus: identifying, assessing and—through planned learning —helping develop the key competencies (knowledge, skill, attitudes) which enable individuals to perform current or future jobs.

ORGANIZATION DEVELOPMENT
focus: assuring healthy inter- and intra-unit relationships and helping groups initiate and manage change.

ORGANIZATION/ JOB DESIGN
focus: defining how tasks, authority and systems will be organized and integrated across organization units and in individual jobs.

UNION/LABOR RELATIONS
focus: assuring healthy union/ organization relationships.

EMPLOYEE ASSISTANCE
focus: providing personal problem-solving, counseling to individual employees.

Human Resource Areas Improved/Increased:
♦ **Quality of work life**
♦ **Productivity**
♦ **HR satisfaction**
♦ **HR development**
♦ **Readiness for change**

HUMAN RESOURCE PLANNING
focus: determining the organization's major human resource needs, strategies and philosophies.

COMPENSATION/ BENEFITS
focus: assuring compensation and benefits fairness and consistency.

PERSONNEL RESEARCH & INFORMATION SYSTEMS
focus: assuring a personnel information base.

SELECTION & STAFFING
focus: matching people and their career needs and capabilities with jobs and career paths.

© The American Society for Training and Development, Washington, DC, 1982.

The performance-based psychological theories of B. F. Skinner at Harvard University had a significant impact on training practices that were designed both to control human behavior and to bring about behavioral change. Training laboratories of the 1960s used behavior modification techniques, programmed instruction, teaching machines, and training hardware designed to shape and control desirable work-related behaviors.

The 1970s witnessed another behavioral application in HRD with the widespread growth of company assessment centers that "objectively" measured employee management potential. At the same time Malcolm Knowles stressed more humanistic-cognitive approaches to learning. He saw the role of the trainer as the facilitator of the learner's needs, rather than as the controller who sought to shape desired behaviors.

The concepts of organizational development (OD) also gained widespread support during the 1970s, interlinking all areas of business HRD. Organizational development shifted the focus of concern from developing people to one centered on the well-being and efficient operation of the entire organization.

Training and development in the 1980s witnessed the rapid growth of quality circles (based on Japanese models) throughout American business. Computer-based training and interactive video were introduced into many companies. They spread quickly with the increasing availability of personal computers (PCs) and appropriate software. However, entering the 1990s, their major limitation remained the lack of customized, inexpensive training and development software for specific company applications. Undoubtedly this issue will begin to fade as increasingly powerful PCs drastically reduce local software development costs.

Management development during the 1980s and early 1990s also saw the continued use of behavioral models of training. They were considered by many trainers and course designers as constituting the best practices for management development, technical, and educational training programs.

During the Cold War era (1945–1992), training and development programs characterized the workforce as groups of employees under a supervisor (see Figure 1.1). Most workers were viewed as long-term, career-oriented community members. Business emphasized employment stability. Because technology had become more complex and interactive, training began to stress teams and retraining while still emphasizing technical skills. Employees were motivated through raises, promotions, and benefits.

Workforce 2000

By the early 1990s the training and development needs of business had begun undergoing significant dynamic shifts. America won the Cold War by rebuilding and re-equipping former adversaries. However, these new industrial bases produced complex technologies and an organizational versatility that has placed extreme competitive pressures on most U.S. business sectors. As a result many employees at all levels discovered that much of what they had learned in school or on the job was now obsolete. They struggled to master high-tech skills or were forced to seek new employment. Many lamented that supple minds had become more important than supple joints.

Unfortunately many U.S. workers are educationally ill-prepared for this new world of work. In the early 1990s the U.S. Department of Education conducted its first national survey on adult reading, writing, and math skills (called the National Audit of International Literacy Standards). Its devastating results indicated that 90 million Americans lacked the necessary basic educational skills to maximize productivity at their current jobs or to be easily retrained for new, more high-tech employment. The U.S. Commerce Department also issued a report (1992) indicating that these educational skill deficits reduced workplace productivity by at least $300 billion each year. Unless this undereducated workforce is retrained, it may mean that many Americans will become the new peasants of the information age. Low skill, low wage jobs may be their only future.

Until recently such companies as IBM, AT&T, Sears, Xerox, and United Airlines implicitly guaranteed their workers a job for life. In exchange, people gave a company their complete loyalty, often placing it ahead of family or personal needs.

Worldwide economic, competitive, technological, political, and social changes have introduced a new era in which to survive and prosper; thus all businesses must become small, lean, and highly focused. Bureaucracy is being eliminated and middle management is shrinking.

Many business planners now see 250 to 500 people as the optimal work unit. Beyond that size people lose interest in the important touchstone—the customer, who has become the only source of business security. Customer loyalty must be constantly earned through outstanding performance. Business interest in total quality management (TQM) is a quest for a workable strategy that requires consistently better performance from every employee.

The business process reengineering movement of the 1990s is reshaping American business, often through the elimination of many middle managers. But the success of this strategy will largely depend on how well newly empowered supervisors and line workers are educated to maximize their individual talents. Strategic manpower planning requires training programs that are designed to foster workers' abilities to perform complex jobs through the development of abstract thinking, problem-solving, and comprehension skills (cognitive abilities).

Future managers, supervisors, and workers must learn how to rethink new solutions to the old ways of doing business. These total quality management, ISO 9000 (International Organization for Standardization), business process reengineering, team-building programs feature problem-solving, creative-ability, and cognitive-based learning. They are far more complex than past behavioral-based company training, and they will challenge both manager and worker alike to develop leadership for a tomorrow that maintains organizational competitiveness.

The organizational structure of the workforce for the year 2000 will most typically be smaller companies utilizing work teams (see Figure 1.1). An employee will be viewed as a human resource who needs constant development. Individual employment will be very changeable and intermittent, driven by rapidly changing technology and the need for extensive continuing education. The training and development offered will be committed to lifelong learning that copes with these frequent changes. Employee motivation will become vested in these job changes and in enrichment that broadens daily work assignments.

THE FUTURE OF EDUCATION AT WORK

Societal changes in the next decades will be enormous. What are the occupational outlook and the new roles of trainers in the workplace? The entire world is now in the midst of a second industrial/technology revolution. Over the next thirty years, major scientific breakthroughs will significantly alter technology, the workplace, and daily life. International economic competitiveness will de-mand that America create and maintain a world-class, universal-worker educational system. If both employees and organizations are to thrive, training and development must become a force in strategic planning that educates all people to their highest potential. However, too often in contemporary business, "wisdom" and "creativity" are seen as opposites. Many managers view creative people as mavericks who do not quite fit into the corporate culture. They certainly are not the people who should be running the shop!

Yet many of these same managers have embraced quality as the competitive cure-all of the 1990s. A comparison of Crosby's fourteen steps, Deming's fourteen points, and Juran's seven points—all three of whom are experts in quality programs—finds a common call to expand training that promotes employee problem solving on the job. All three call for empowered work teams that can integrate a range of complex thinking tasks into their daily work activities. This quality "continuous improvement process" requires that people make decisions, analyze systems, investigate options, invent new processes, and classify, compare, and generally manipulate information. Increasing personal creativity has become the name of the game for American business.

We believe that most companies need to encourage employee education at all levels. A business that cannot bridge the "business wisdom" to "employee creativity" culture gap will soon experience serious trouble. The worldwide competitive marketplace has already begun this winnowing-out process.

The foundation of America's national wealth is really its human capital—people. Their knowledge, skills, and motivation remain the primary assets of any business. In 1987 William Wiggenhorn, director of training at Motorola, noted, "We've documented the savings for the statistical process-control methods and problem-solving methods we've trained our people in. We're running a rate of return of about thirty times the dollar invested."

To offer this impressive rate of return for more companies, we must prepare more professional trainers for a dramatic increase in the technical retraining needed on an ongoing basis by every business sector. American business must seriously consider offering career education/school-to-work programs through local schools. These training programs will prepare the next generation of young people for the high-tech realities of the twenty-first century workplace.

Most of the modern consumer goods used by every American—the automobile, television, videocassette recorder, compact disc player, tape deck, and so on—were invented in the United States.

Yet almost all of these products are now manufactured overseas because America lacks the technically qualified, educated personnel to make the product in a high-tech, controlled-cost, quality environment. Who will make the next generation of high-tech products: high-definition television (HDTV); hypersonic aircraft; battery-driven cars; smaller, faster, more powerful computers? Will those products be invented in America only to be manufactured in Korea, Singapore, or Germany?

Sixty-six percent of all German employees are certified graduates of their youth training system. About 596,000 (as of 1992) German teenagers between the ages of fifteen and nineteen participate in this program. Overall 1.6 million apprentices (6.5 percent of the labor force) undertake a two-to-three-year job preparation program in any one of some 380 occupations. The cost to German industry in 1991 was about $10,500 per apprentice. Does the system benefit business? One indicator is that businesses offer 22 percent more apprenticeship slots than there are applicants.

One reason for this broad support is that the apprentice system is so well established throughout Germany that companies are not afraid of having workers poached. German unions do not severely limit student apprenticeships to create artificial shortages of skilled workers. Senior German management recognizes that profits and productivity are a direct result of a strategic, long-term investment in lifelong employee education. Five hundred thousand companies (mostly small businesses) invest $40 billion in the German youth apprenticeship program. An additional $40 billion is allocated by these companies to train their current adult workers.

Whether U.S. businesses will respond with similar programs is yet to be seen. Scattered company efforts have already started across the United States. One thing is certain; we must train our trainers on how to successfully collaborate with local educational institutions if our effort is to succeed. If other countries can do this, why not the United States?

The $50-billion-a-year corporate training budget of U.S. companies sounds impressive. But it is only a fraction of America's annual corporate capital hardware bill, which runs about $400 billion each year. Motorola is not a nationwide industrial leader by accident. Employee education is at the heart of both its short-term and long-term planning.

America is pretty much in the same position as it was at the beginning of the nineteenth century. At that time there was a gradual realization by business, union, and government leaders that a fundamental change was required in America's basic business agenda. The United States sensed it could not compete with a rapidly industrializing Europe unless the average American worker was literate and had vocational skills. Between 1890 and 1920, American society embarked on the difficult task of introducing sweeping educational reforms.

There was tremendous opposition by some in business to mandatory public education. Child labor was cheap; schooling would drive up business costs. However, the new technology of the early twentieth century demanded a realistic partnership between business and labor that enacted into law America's first educational revolution. The time has now dawned for a second effort. The demands of the marketplace have far outpaced the schoolhouse's ability to educate the majority of our children for life beyond 2001.

A widespread national consensus is being mobilized for significant change both in the schoolhouse and in the corporate classroom. Diverse groups across America are demanding basic educational reform for all people, young and old. A second American education revolution may unfold.

No matter what the eventual scenario of the second American education revolution, it will not reach completion overnight. Even drastically improved public education is incapable by itself of supporting America's industrial competitiveness. Of equal importance is quickly establishing a corporate policy that expands the role of employee education within all businesses, both large and small.

It is up to training professionals to help senior managers understand that planning includes investing in employee workforce education through expanded company training and development programs. The realization of these twin strategic objectives—national education reform and local company workforce education programs—will help America regain lost productivity and international competitive advantage in almost every business sector.

As part of a company's strategic business plan, management needs to reconsider training by assessing its total workforce's skills. What are the employees' educational skill levels in relation to domestic and foreign competition? Is this educational skill gap increasing or decreasing versus key competitors? In many instances individual businesses will find that they are far behind in the education and training they will need to offer all their employees for the ultra-modern, post-twentieth-century marketplace.

However, the experience of too many managers is that training is "not worth what I've paid." Employees go and listen and say it was wonderful, and they do it for a while, only eventually to forget it and go back to their old habits. Training is useless unless change occurs and becomes part of a process that awakens people to their own strengths and weaknesses.

In the 1980s many new adult learning strategies were discovered for stimulating thinking and intelligence. Frederick Goodwin, director of the National Institute of Mental Health, believes that educational programs cannot make a 70 IQ person into a 120 IQ person. "But you can change their IQ in different ways, perhaps as much as 20 points up or down, based on their environment." There are many untapped abstract reasoning capabilities that currently are not being developed by traditional business training/educational programs.

We offer the Workforce Education Triad as a potential occupational model for the future of careers in education at work (see Figure 1.3). Companies will continue to offer training in basic management, supervision, service, and assembly behaviors. They will add a component for employee skill requirements that increases overall personal comprehension: writing, math, reading, foreign language, and English as a second language. Only after addressing these two employee development areas will a business be able to successfully address the education issues of building higher thinking skills for TQM, ISO 9000, business process re-engineering, work teams, problem solving, personal creativity, and advanced technical or professional education.

Business will also need to tie in to their workforce development program joint collaboration for career education and school-to-work programs with local educational institutions. This includes elementary, secondary, and postsecondary institutions. Only in this way will businesses be able to develop the future high-tech employees they will need for a high-productivity, world-class, competitive workplace.

America now stands at an economic crossroads. One path leads to a continued decline in the standard of living and sees the United States eclipsed as the world's leading economic power. The other road leads toward FutureWork—a fundamental restructuring of American business for 2001 and beyond.

The Cold War is over, but an international competitive war has begun. America has proven it can resist invading armies; but will business and political leaders recognize the new economic course charted by the world's industrial community? In the late-twentieth century, international business investment in human capital has emerged as the single most important business strategy to attain and retain a significant competitive economic advantage.

The authors believe that better educating all adults with the Workforce Education Triad is an attainable goal for every busi-

Figure 1.3.   The Workforce Education Triad

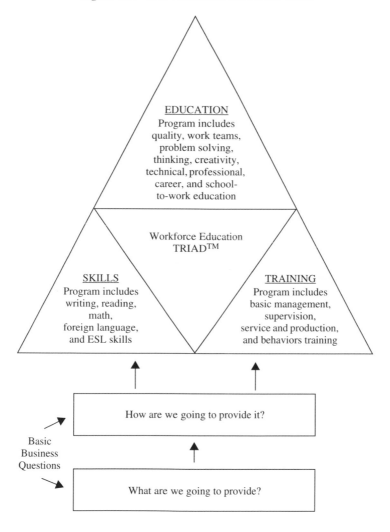

ness, large or small. Aging may slow people down somewhat, but if adults can control the pace of learning, and if hearing and visual problems are corrected, people have the same ability to learn in their fifties as they had in their twenties. This continues to be true until old age, sometimes even after the age of seventy.

Everywhere the new global marketplace is undermining the nation-state as the fundamental socially integrating force. This new international economy now benefits only 20 percent of American workers. The other 80 percent are economically standing still or falling behind. Well-educated Americans typically work in office buildings. These "glass-tower people" are linked to their counterparts in Germany and Japan. Their economy is upward bound. Unfortunately, too many of their undereducated fellow Americans are not heading in the same direction.

Unless this basic socioeconomic condition is corrected, the United States will become a two-tier economic society. A well-educated, economically mobile upper class will be dwarfed in numbers by a large, poorly educated economic underclass that lacks the educational ability to function in a high-tech, glass-tower business environment. This means the end of the American economic system as we have known it and perhaps a severe disruption of our society as the average standard of living sinks out of sight. This is too high a price to pay for our lack of agreement on a new social agenda for the reform of American education in school and at work.

The authors believe that future career opportunities in training and development will largely be based on the Workforce Education Triad of training, skills, and education. For the rest of the 1990s, maximizing the talents of all people is emerging as a major business goal. How you might fit into this workplace learning revolution will be presented in the following chapters.

CHAPTER 2

TRAINING & DEVELOPMENT AS AN ORGANIZATION

WHAT TRAINERS DO

The various tasks that training professionals perform are based on a number of variables, including the size of the organization in which they work as well as the organizational goals and objectives. In addition the trainer brings personal skills and knowledge to the organization. Given these many variables trainers may be responsible for a wide variety of roles including:

- needs analysis and diagnosis
- determining training strategies
- program planning and design
- developing materials
- managing resources, internal and external
- delivering training
- on-the-job training (OJT)
- coaching
- organizational development
- individual development
- research
- managing the training function
- self-development

In performing these responsibilities, a trainer might be called upon to undertake some or all of the following assignments:

- reading business plans
- talking to people involved in developing plans
- analyzing jobs and functions
- analyzing changes and how they affect jobs/functions
- analyzing performance problems
- designing a curriculum
- managing projects
- developing budgets
- scheduling
- developing graphics
- developing video or computer-based modules
- conducting a pilot program
- delivering a training program
- diagnosing learning difficulties
- coaching
- assessing, administering tests
- providing feedback
- determining a trainee's mastery of objectives
- determining a trainee's transfer of skills/knowledge to the job
- calculating the cost/value of training
- writing reports
- measuring results
- conducting research

The day-to-day roles and responsibilities of a trainer are largely driven by his or her specific organization's beliefs and values about training. Discovering the answers to the following basic questions about a company will provide you with some very valuable information.

1. What role does training play in ensuring business performance?
2. What is training expected to accomplish?
3. What is the expectation of supervisors/managers?

4. Is training considered an investment or an expense?
5. Is continual learning and improvement a core value?
6. What responsibility does an individual employee have?

An ideal training system is an integrated set of processes that interact to produce business results. This includes five important components: an overall structure that governs the work of training; multileveled planning; quality operations (design and delivery of training programs); formal results reporting; backup processes (registration, scheduling, facilities, manuals, organizational structure, financial resources, and so forth). Your information assessment of the structure of the training function within an organization should be based on these five essential areas. Completing this process will help you target the strengths and weaknesses of an organization's training system.

TRAINING PROGRAM DESIGN/DEVELOPMENT

The responsibility for the design and development of training programs is the role of a variety of professionals. The primary role for development is in the hands of a program planner, also called program developer, instructional designer, or training specialist. Those in this position work with subject matter experts, supervisors, managers, administrators, and/or department heads in a collaborative relationship.

A program planner acts as the training process expert and/or manager of the program planning process. An essential element in the process is establishing support for the program. In many organizations there are specific key people who are continually tapped for support. For example, the supervisor of the program's participants can be invaluable in the following:

- assisting in the assessment of needs
- assisting in scheduling training sessions
- reviewing materials
- collecting baseline data

- attending parts of the program
- serving as a resource person or instructor
- providing informal feedback on how the program was received
- helping participants connect what they are learning in the program to their jobs
- encouraging participants to share with peers what they have learned
- collecting data for follow-up programs

In addition to seeking the active involvement of supervisors before, during, and after the program, developers also need to assist supervisors with the transfer of learning into the actual work experience.

Senior management's support of the training function—or lack of it—is most often reflected in its budgetary commitment to and public support of training in organization publications and key organization meetings. They can help by publicizing the successful results and benefits of the training programs. Management needs to develop formal policies and procedures concerning training and development activities. You can also ask selected managers/administrators to become involved in the design of highly visible programs.

Another successful strategy is to establish ownership for training. To do this you might:

- identify organization problems and issues for which training might offer solutions
- assist in conducting a needs analysis
- assist in defining program objectives
- review program design drafts
- present training results and achievements to senior managers
- help locate resources
- actively endorse policies and procedures that support quality training

IDENTIFYING NEEDS

Unless a specific training program is mandated as a federal regulation, conducting a needs analysis is one of the best ways of involving people in planning training activities. There is no one accepted best method or process for conducting a formal needs assessment as an organized way to identify specific training needs.

The focus of assessment is to clarify and define problems, not solutions. Because there are endless ways to gather information, the best methods to use are those that produce accurate information. In most cases a variety of methods can be used that already fit into an organization's way of doing business. Data gathering methods useful in conducting a needs assessment might include:

1. Observations—watching workers doing tasks, jobs
2. Written questionnaires/surveys—gathering opinions, attitudes, and perceptions in writing
3. Interviews—talking with people in person or on the phone
4. Group sessions—brainstorming, participating in focus groups, taking consensus
5. Job and task analysis—collecting data from a variety of people who know a job (incumbent, supervisor, manager, customer)
6. Paper-pencil tests—using a diagnostic tool to measure workers' knowledge, skills, and attitudes
7. Written information—utilizing reports, policies, procedure manuals, employee records, professional standards, and legislation
8. Informally talking to people—recording and checking out ideas and information

There are two aspects to the process of gathering this information: selecting people to answer the questions and selecting people to ask them. Program designers, with the help of others, then translate the ideas that have been identified in the needs assessment into priority needs for training programs.

It is important to understand that education and training are not always the answer to all the ideas and problems identified during the needs assessment process. However, trainers still have a responsibility for developing and/or initiating any alternative business interventions. Such alternatives might include:

1. Job aids—supply directions for doing a work task that are simple, concrete, and provide a quick reference.
2. Redefinition of job/task—provide performance standards, job enrichment, and job rotation.
3. Feedback system—develop a process for providing information to individuals/group through team meetings and memos.
4. Personnel practices—change methods of recruitment, screening, hiring, training, and rewarding.
5. Changes in work environment, facilities, tasks—provide the proper conditions or tools used to do a job.
6. Organizational development—formulate a plan for improving the organization.

As you can see, sorting the information collected is a critical step in the needs analysis process. The trainer, by analyzing, condensing, and organizing these data, begins to develop business recommendations around specific business issues, some of which will probably include nontraining issues.

DEVELOPING PROGRAM OBJECTIVES

Program objectives, based on your training needs assessment, are then ready to be written. These should be clear statements of the anticipated results to be achieved through a training program. Ideally, objectives will specify the skills and knowledge to be developed in individual jobs and how these skills will impact on workers' performance. They will also show how applying these skills will affect business operations and how the expected operational results will meet corporate objectives.

An example for a program's objectives might look like this:

Corporate Goal	Increase market share of product X by reducing number of customer complaints.
Line Manager Goal	Reduce customer complaints by 25 percent
Training Objectives	Produce error free orders within 24 hours. Ask specific, clarifying questions of customer when necessary.

Program objectives must focus on what trainees will learn by participating in the training program. They should be measurable and applicable to the work setting. Objectives also serve as the primary guidepost for the program evaluation process.

Collecting evaluation data occurs before, during, and after the program. Before the program, baseline data indicate the participants' current knowledge, skills, attitude, and/or information relative to procedures and operations. During the program, data are produced on participants' learning through observation, conversations, assessment, and questionnaires. At the end of the training program, changes in the participants' knowledge level and skill performance can be assessed, a cost-benefit analysis (economic value-added) can be made, and personal employee performance reviews can be further honed.

Program objectives may focus on the acquisition of knowledge, the enhancement of thinking skills, the development of psychomotor skills, or a change in personal attitudes and values. These objectives are stated in terms of what adult learners will be able to know, do, and feel as a result of participation in the training.

Program objectives consist of:

1. An opening statement—"The learner will be able to" (plus an action verb) "demonstrate."
2. A description of the subject being taught—"the correct sequence in installing program A."

Examples:

A. The learner will be able to demonstrate the correct sequence in installing program A.
B. The learner will be able to describe the five approved methods for handling customer complaints.

PROGRAM CONTENT

Selecting the content of a training program should be based on clear training objectives. Carefully identifying these objectives is essential to their successful achievement. Because of a trainer's time constraints, this can be a difficult step. Trainers must be careful to neither leave out important points and ideas, nor overemphasize secondary issues.

The order or sequence in which the training content is delivered is another significant consideration. How this is accomplished rests on the level of the trainee's prior knowledge, his or her personal experiences, and the nature of the content itself. For example, a trainer must begin a course sequence with familiar materials rather than new information, or with a framework that helps trainees organize what they are learning. A course could easily present learned tasks first, as well as broad concepts that apply throughout different course sequences.

TRAINING METHODS

A critical step in designing a training program is choosing the instructional techniques that best fit the specific content. The course developer considers the following learning strategies when making this decision:

- Acquisition of knowledge—lecture, group discussion, group exercise, buzz
- Thinking skills—case studies, critical incidents, games, simulations
- Psychomotor skills—demonstration with return demonstration by participants, skill drill
- Attitude change—group discussions, role playing, exercises, games

PROGRAM EVALUATION

Program evaluation is not a one-shot event. Instead it is an ongoing process. Curriculum measures, in the form of pre- and post-tests or exercises, provide the instructor with information about participants' knowledge-skill base both prior to the program and after the program. Evaluation involves the assessment of the quality of the program, the delivery of the program by the instructor, and the effectiveness of the transfer of learning to the workplace.

The final aspect of program design, which is often ignored, is communicating the results of a training program. The Training Evaluation Pyramid (see Figure 2.1) summarizes these assessment options: measuring audience reaction, determining the degree of trainee learning, evaluating changes in employee behavior back on the job, and assessing the economic value added (EVA) by a training program (return on investment).

TRAINING PROGRAM IMPLEMENTATION

Program trainers will either have developed the training program or will use a program already developed by someone else. In either case this trainer is responsible for the program's implementation. In some cases the trainer is also responsible for the logistics of the program; this requires attention to details and the ability to keep track of numerous tasks in a timely manner. The larger the program the more important it is to spend the time and effort needed before, during, and after its implementation to make sure it runs smoothly. For example, making sure there is adequate classroom space for the training is essential in order to facilitate the entire learning experience. In organizing facilities trainers need to

Figure 2.1.   Training Evaluation Pyramid

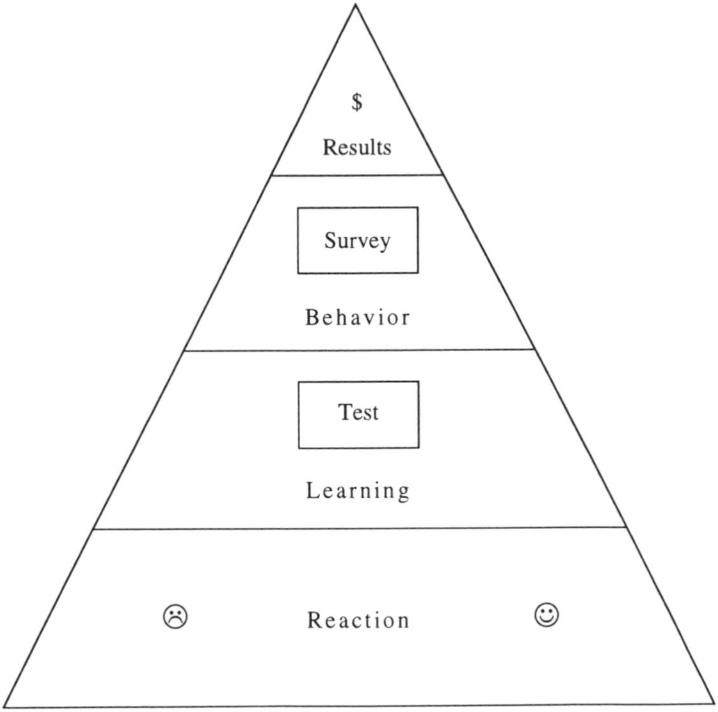

Source: Gordon, Edward E., Ronald R. Morgan, and Judith A. Ponticell. *Future Work: The Revolution Reshaping American Business.* Praeger, 1994.

keep in mind room arrangements and instructional equipment. Keeping a checklist is imperative when organizing the many activities and issues involved in implementing a training program.

TRAIN-THE-TRAINER WORKSHOPS

The technology and information explosions occurring within organizations make it more critical than ever that employees perform their jobs optimally to help their business stay competitive, productive, and profitable. The training department is the educational resource whose goal is to serve internal customers as effectively as possible in creating a high-performance organization.

Many companies use content experts as trainers, or they may use managers, supervisors, or professionals who are nontrainers by education and experience but who are experts in their field. Content experts understand business issues, have real-world experience in their field, possess current knowledge of its tools, and need shorter preparation time before training delivery. However, the risk involved in using content experts is their inexperience as trainers/adult educators. In this case, basic communication, presentation, and group facilitation skills can be offered through train-the-trainer workshops. Also content experts need to be aware of how adults go through the learning process in order to increase individual trainee motivation.

Today we know more about how to train than ever before. This knowledge has led to the development of train-the-trainer seminars and workshops that are presented by a variety of training companies and organizations. These seminars/workshops vary from a one-day Fred Pryor seminar to a four-and-one-half-day American Management Association seminar. The purpose of train-the-trainer seminars is to help the participants develop critical training competencies that they can use effectively. The content of most programs is similar; what varies is the depth of information presented and the opportunity to practice the skills learned with critical feedback, including the videotaping of presentations. (See Figure 2.2.)

Train-the-trainers seminars focus on the instructional techniques needed to become a dynamic trainer. They are geared toward instructors rather than designers, but most include some basic design information such as writing objectives, determining and sequencing content, developing exercises, and using instructional methodologies. The content of these seminars can be broken down into the categories of principles of learning, program management, and delivery skills.

The *principles of learning* segment usually begins with the concept of adult learning, which includes how adults learn. Motivation is discussed as well as tips for making material interesting and keeping learners enthusiastic and energized. Feedback and review methods are also important topics. Most programs include retention principles and what to do when learners do not understand the material presented.

Program management covers the physical arrangement, size, and audiovisual equipment requirements of the training room. This segment also provides techniques for handling difficult participants, maintaining control of problem situations, and improving group dynamic skills.

The *delivery skills* segment of the seminar concentrates on improving the verbal and nonverbal presentation style of participants. Learners are exposed to techniques for promoting participation, leading a discussion, asking the best type of questions, using audiovisual aids to enhance presentations, and conducting small-group exercises. Most programs also include time for participants to practice their delivery skills while they are being videotaped. Each taped presentation is followed with a critique by the instructor and/or peers. Later, participants can review their tape and assess their presentations, focusing on improving a specific skill on which they need to work. Videotaping presentations documents the progress of participants and builds their self-confidence.

Figure 2.2. Train-the-Trainer Programs

Content	Providers				
	A	B	C	D	E
Adult Learning Principles	x	x	x	x	x
Analyzing Training Needs	x	x		x	x
Application on-the-Job				x	x
Verbal Communication	x	x	x	x	x
Nonverbal Communication	x	x	x	x	x
Developing and Using Training Aids	x	x	x	x	x
Evaluation, Feedback	x	x	x	x	x
Facilitation Skills	x	x	x	x	x
Follow-up	x			x	x
Handling Problem Participants	x	x	x	x	x
Identifying and Sequencing Content	x	x	x	x	x
Individual Learning Styles	x		x	x	x
Learning Climate	x		x	x	x
Objectives	x		x	x	x
Measuring Results	x		x	x	x
Practice	x	x		x	x
Presentation Skills	x	x		x	x
Selecting Best Methods	x		x	x	x
Videotaping with Critiques	x	x			x

Providers	# Days	1995–96 Cost
A = Language in Learning Services, Ontario, Canada	3	$899.00
B = University Associates, Tucson, Arizona	2	$765.00
C = Fred Pryor Seminars, Shawnee Mission, Kansas	1	$149.00
D = University of Wisconsin, Madison, Wisconsin	3	$825.00
E = American Management Association	4½	$1695.00

PRESENTATION SKILLS

There is nothing as important to the success of a well developed training program than a trainer who is prepared and has mastered essential presentation skills. Every trainer can prepare; however, mastering presentation skills requires practice, practice, and more practice. The skills essential to becoming a successful, effective presenter include the ability to:

- communicate clearly and logically
- establish a learning climate
- establish rapport with a group
- use appropriate gestures and body language to communicate nonverbally
- make eye contact with participants and rotate attention throughout the group
- use questioning techniques
- use active listening techniques
- use motivational techniques to keep learners excited about the learning process
- stimulate group discussions by asking probing questions
- involve the group through the use of exercises, case studies, demonstrations, role playing
- use a variety of training methodologies
- "read" and react to a group
- summarize material
- give clear, specific, task-oriented directions
- maintain group interest
- know how and when to use a variety of visuals
- handle questions asked by participants
- show enthusiasm for the learning taking place
- use training techniques appropriately: group exercises, hand-outs, overheads, flipcharts, role playing, games

- evaluate training throughout the session
- organize presentation and materials
- observe participants
- provide feedback to the group and individuals
- be flexible
- provide for follow up
- manage training time
- know the organization or business
- maintain control of group behavior
- effectively handle difficult participants

THE TRAINING LEADER

The most important responsibility of the person managing the training is to demonstrate the usefulness of training in achieving the goals and objectives of the organization. In order to handle this primary responsibility, the training manager must understand his or her organization's goals, priorities, and values. In other words, the training manager must know and live the strategic plan that senior management has determined for the future of the company. The training managers and employees need to meet their company's goals. This requires strong leadership skills, and the training manager determines the value training adds to the organization.

The training department will always be involved in addressing the skills needed to perform specific jobs within an organization. Historically training departments have done this well. But the broader responsibility of training as a support to management and to the performance of the organization as a whole means both establishing direct communication with senior management and keeping an eye on change in order to serve new strategic priorities.

Training managers must sell the benefits of what they accomplish and find quantifiable data to analyse a situation before and after training. Bottom line training results need to show how much change has occurred. Trainers need to publish these results on an ongoing basis to consistently demonstrate a picture of organization change through training aligned to the vision of the organization's top management.

For example, Bob Dust, president of Gyrus Systems, Inc., recommends using training records to determine the following for previous years:

AVERAGE TRAINING HOURS PER EMPLOYEE. This measures the quantity of training and tells how productive training has been as a function of time. When correlated to job title or department, it can highlight areas that need some attention.

AVERAGE TRAINING COST PER EMPLOYEE. This measures the average benefit cost training represents for employees. This can be broken down by EEO [Equal Employment Opportunity], class, job status, job title and organization structure to determine what each group of employees is receiving.

TOTAL INSTRUCTION HOURS. This measures the supply of classrooms and how much they are used. It helps plan classroom load and requirements for future training. It also indicates how much time is spent delivering training as opposed to developing and promoting it. Looked at from the viewpoint of instructors, it tracks their workload, too.

TOTAL CLASS HOURS. This measures how many hours are spent in all training, including instructor-led, self-study, and external training.

COST OF STUDENT ABSENCES. This measures the cost of students who registered for a program but did not attend. In the world of business this is considered "spoiled inventory," inventory that has been paid for, but was discarded.

STUDENT ENROLLMENT/CLASS CAPACITY. This is a form of excess inventory measurement. If the optimum size of a program is 10 and the program costs $4,500 to present, the per person cost is $450. If only nine students show up the cost jumps to $500, reducing your return on investment.

WAIT LISTED/ENROLLMENT. This measures unsatisfied demand; too high a number indicates the supply of training is deficient. As the number reaches zero, the supply is too high.

Source: *Measure the Training Department's Success with Business Statistics.* Gyrus Systems, Inc., June 1955.

There is no "best" organizational structure for training and education. The culture of each organization dictates what structure will work to achieve the goals established. Some training departments are a part of human resources, marketing, or sales; others are independent departments equal to other major departments. No organizational structure will fit all situations. In fact, even within companies with a training structure that currently works, there must be room for changes that are a part of the evolution of any organization.

Svenson and Rinderer present an ideal training system, one that shows training as an integrated set of systems and processes that interact to produce results. Their model (see Figure 2.3) includes:

Governance. The overall structure of committees and councils that oversee the work of the training organization.

Planning. The hierarchy of planning at all levels that drives the work of the training organization forward.

Operations. That part of the training system that is most often meant when we think of training.

Results. The system that tells us how well we are doing.

Support. The system that provides all the backup processes.

Figure 2.3.   The Training System

GOVERNANCE				
Executive Board of Education	Functional Curriculum Councils	Training Administration Council	Project Committees	Organizational Unit Training Committees

PLANNING					
Strategic Training Plans	Annual Training Plan and Budget	Organizational Unit Training Plans	Individual Training Plans	Project Plans	Delivery Plans and Schedules

OPERATIONS					
Needs Analysis	Curriculum Architecture	Instructional Design/ Development	Delivery	On-the-Job Application	Maintenance

RESULTS					
Overall Performance	Trainee Opinions	Mastery Testing	Transfer of Learning to Job Performance	Impact on Business Results	Financial Results

SUPPORT					
Information System	Registration and Scheduling	Communi- cations	Production Support	Facilities	Technologies
Specialists' Support	Administra- tive Manuals	Organization Structure	Financial Systems	External Resources	Supervisor/ Manager Staffing

Source: Svenson, Raynold A. and Monica J. Rinderer. *The Training & Development Strategic Plan Workbook.* Prentice-Hall, 1992.

THE FACILITATOR AS CHANGE AGENT

Before we can design a more open, creative business learning model, we must reconsider the role of our primary change agent, the trainer. We need to move most business-related teachers, instructors, and trainers from their current presentation mode toward a facilitator/mentoring role model (see Figure 2.4). Unless we train the trainer to become a cognitive facilitator, our newly designed models will fail. Here is why.

Traditional classroom teachers, instructors (technical training), and company management trainers view their students or trainees as passive learning agents (see Figure 2.4) to whom they present or demonstrate new information. In their expert role they seek to shape effective learner behaviors. They focus on learning concepts, new skills, or practical how-to knowledge. The traditional educator makes the learning process meaningful and helps the learner achieve a new level of understanding, adopt a new technique, or acquire the desired effective behavior by using rewards. These developmental educational roles can be compared with the characteristics of the behaviorally based learning models referred to in Chapter 1.

The desirable alternative is a facilitator/mentor, cognitive-change agent model. The focus shifts to the adult learner as an active participant rather than a passive attendee. The facilitator becomes a helper in the discovery process. This role supersedes, but does not completely eliminate, aspects of the behaviorally based models. Content is mastered through discovery learning, which gives added personal meaning to each adult rather than filling his or her mind with facts, skills, or behaviors. The learning process has meaning because it is built around the individual's work/life instead of the educator's interpretations. The bottom line outcomes are the personally learned discoveries that the adult can

Figure 2.4. Developmental Education Role Models

	ROLE	TRAINEE	ROLE VIS-À-VIS "HELPEES"	CONTENT EMPHASIS	LOCUS OF MEANING	DESIRED OUTCOMES
CHANGE AGENT	Facilitator/Mentor	Participants	Helper in a Discovery Process	Inductive Learning	Individual "Explorers"	Discovery and Application
	Trainer	Trainees	Shaper of Effective Behavior	Skill Acquisition	In the Trainer	Effective Behavior
TRADI-TIONAL	Instructor (Technical Training)	Students	Expert and Demonstrator	'How to …'	In Definition of Effectiveness	Strategy, Tactics, and Technique
	Teacher	Students	Imparter of Information and Meaning	Conceptual Understanding	In the Teacher's Interpretation	Awareness and Understanding

DIMENSION

Source: Adapted from Jones, J. E. and M. Woodcock. *The Manual of Management Development*. Aldershot, UK: Gower Publishers, 1985, p. 113.

apply on the job today and adapt tomorrow to changed work assignments. This facilitator/mentor role is the central determinant of success supporting a new thinking and problem-solving training design. It supports the characteristics we have established for successful cognitively based business learning models.

To use this change agent model, several specific design elements must be addressed in a training program.

> To accept new material, adult learners have a need to know "what's in it for me."

> Most adult learners have personal experiences that will give meaning to their learning of new ideas.

> It is far easier for participants to accept a new concept if they are involved in its development during the training process.

> If the facilitator can state something, why not have the facilitator ask the participants to help develop the same information from their own perspectives by asking open-ended questions?

> The facilitator builds the participants into subject-matter experts and does not remain the sole source of knowledge.

> Participants' responses are never completely wrong. Some piece of their idea may be linked to the desired training application or principle, or the facilitator can extend the participant's thinking and build upon it.

> The primary task of any facilitator is to develop maximum learner participation and understanding.

> To implement what has been learned, a primary task for all participants and their managers is to formulate a personal action plan for the workplace.

CHAPTER 3

A PROFILE OF THE TRAINING FIELD

No single profile can describe a typical job in the field of training and human resource development. Training and development professionals are a heterogeneous group with varied backgrounds, skills, and responsibilities. Some are employees of the corporations in which they train. Some are external consultants. Many are generalists. Others have any of a wide variety of specialties, including management development, technical training, sales training, organization development, career development, quality or performance improvement, and organization or job design. The tasks they perform include administering, evaluating, and managing HRD programs and services; analyzing learning needs; developing, marketing, or delivering instructional materials; designing programs; and serving as agents for organizational change.

What do they have in common? They all use training, HRD, organizational development, or career development in their efforts to improve the effectiveness of individuals, groups, and organizations. And they are all members of a dynamic, constantly evolving profession that offers many rewards to its practitioners.

Among the most tangible rewards in any field are the financial ones. In the first section of this chapter, we'll look at salaries and other forms of compensation for training specialists in various jobs, organizations, and locations. But money isn't everything. Working conditions can also mean the difference between a career you love and a job you hate. The second section of this chapter will discuss working conditions for trainers in different settings.

Sometimes job satisfaction is based on more subjective elements. Trainers describe a spectrum of personal motivations that attract people to the field and keep them there. The chapter will conclude with a look at the less tangible reasons for choosing a career in training and development.

COMPENSATION

Salaries and other compensation for training and development professionals vary widely. A recent salary survey, conducted by *Training* magazine (November 1995), revealed that 57 percent of trainers believe they are underpaid. But a few top earners in the field actually make as much as $250,000 a year, according to a survey by Abbot, Langer & Associates.

Who makes that kind of money? In the May 1995 issue of *Training & Development* magazine, Rebecca Thomas describes a composite profile, based on the survey results (see Figure 3.1). The typical top earner is a corporate HRD director who manages ten or more professional-level employees and has an advanced degree. According to the survey report, he or she is most likely to work in a manufacturing firm in one of the following industries: aerospace; fabricated metal; food, beverage, or tobacco; and stone, clay, glass, or concrete. Other highly paid training and development professionals work in merchandising firms or utilities with 10,000 or more employees or annual sales of $250 million or more.

The Bottom Line on Training Salaries

Of course, most training and development specialists will never reach the six-figure mark. The average gross annual salary of the 1,802 respondents to the *Training* magazine survey was quite a bit

---

Figure 3.1.   Average Salaries in Seven HRD Job Categories

Classroom Instructor
$42,076

Instructional Designer
$44,206

One-Person Training Department
$44,431

Specialist in Management, Career,
or Organizational Development
$46,753

Manager of Training or HRD
(supervising 1 to 4 full-time trainers)
$51,167

Manager of Training or HRD
(supervising 5 or more full-time trainers)
$59,178

Executive-Level Manager
of Training or HRD
$69,267

Source: *Training* magazine, November 1995. Salaries cited are annual. Results are compiled from 1,802 respondents.

lower than that, at $50,400. Even those results are not representative of the field as a whole. The *Training* study included a disproportionate number of higher-level trainers: 80 percent of respondents were managers or one-person training departments. And 24 percent had at least thirteen years of experience in the training field.

The 1994–1995 *Occupational Outlook Handbook,* published by the U.S. Department of Labor, lists a median annual salary of $32,000 for human resource specialists in 1992. It describes a range that starts at $17,000 for the lowest-paid specialists and tops out at $64,000 for the highest-paid managers. Keep in mind that the *Occupational Outlook Handbook* does not break training out into a separate section but puts it under the human resources umbrella that includes other human resource specialties such as labor relations, personnel, position classification, and affirmative action.

Factors affecting a training specialist's salary, not surprisingly, include education, experience level, performance record, job category, geographic location, and the type and size of the organization. For example, according to the *Occupational Outlook Handbook,* starting salaries for bachelor's degree graduates in human resources averaged $22,900 in 1993; for master's degree recipients, the average was $30,500.

The *Training* survey results don't include starting salaries, but they do break down the data by position and by years of experience in the training field. Classroom instructor was the lowest-paid job title in the study. The average salary for instructors with three or fewer years of experience was $34,993; for those with thirteen or more years of experience, it was $48,366. Compare that to average salaries for executive-level training and HRD managers: $61,278 for those with three or fewer years of experience and $74,465 for the thirteen-plus group.

The *Occupational Outlook Handbook* lists average salaries for selected job descriptions, using data from the Abbott, Langer & Associates survey. Most of the occupations cited are personnel-related rather than training-related. But the report does include an average annual salary for corporate training directors of $63,900.

Not surprisingly, the largest, most financially secure firms pay their training professionals higher salaries than those paid by smaller firms. In *Training*'s survey, organizations with gross sales or assets of $500 million or more paid respondents, on average, $56,700 a year. Respondents who work for employers with sales or assets between $20 million and $500 million made $50,457. And those whose employers had sales or assets under $20 million averaged $43,363. The highest-paying employers tended to be those in the areas of transportation, communication, and utilities; manufacturing; and the wholesale and retail trades (see Figure 3.2).

Geographic region also plays a part in determining levels of compensation. The Northeast, with its relatively high cost of living, led the United States in trainers' salaries, with an average $54,006 a year for respondents to *Training*'s survey. The west central region—roughly, the Rocky Mountain states—came in at the bottom of the list, with an average of $45,900. In general employers on both coasts and in the Great Lakes region paid a little more than those in the central part of the country.

Figure 3.2.   Average Salaries for Trainers, by Industry

Transportation, communications, and utilities
$54,525

Manufacturing
$52,788

Wholesale or retail trade
$51,714

Educational services
$50,608

Business services
$48,828

Finance, insurance, and banking
$48,825

Health services
$45,942

Public administration
$44,477

Average in all industries
$50,400

Source: *Training* magazine, November 1995. Salaries cited are annual. Results are compiled from 1,802 respondents.

Consultants: Writing Your Own Ticket

Not all HRD professionals work in-house as corporate training and development specialists. What about those who have eschewed life on the inside in exchange for the freedom of running their own consulting firms? How much do independent consultants make? Unfortunately there is no simple answer. "Don't expect this kind of information to fall into your lap," caution Marilyn Corrigan and Sally Sparhawk in *Info-Line 9403: Becoming an Outside Consultant.* "People are generally very closed-mouth about fees. You will have to do a lot of digging and experimenting to discover what you are really worth on the market."

Theoretically, the amount of money you can make as an independent consultant is limitless. It depends not only on the fees you set, but also on the type of consulting you do, the going rate in your part of the country (or a client's part of the country), the amount of work you are willing to put in, your experience and contacts, and your reputation as someone who gets results.

You want to keep your rates low enough to attract clients. But you shouldn't sell yourself short. Not only do you need to bring in a reasonable income; you also must cover the costs of running your business. And many buyers of consulting services say they're wary of consultants who charge too little! It's not always true that you get what you pay for, but some clients assume that a cut-rate consultant will give bargain-basement-quality service.

So how can you predict what you could make as a consultant?

Most training consultants base their rates on a daily fee. In its August 1994 issue, *Training & Development* reports the results of an admittedly unscientific poll (the sample was self-selected) on what independent consultants are paid and what they're worth. Consultants were asked about their highest daily rates. Most respondents (51 percent) said they charged between $1,000 and $2,000. But some set their fees more creatively. A Montana-based consultant said he often barters his services—he has consulted in exchange for golf games, motel stays, computers, clothing, and even a side of beef!

Training & Development's July 1990 issue provided a forum for four anonymous consultants to talk about their prices. When asked about setting his daily rates, one of the four consultants was candid: "Arbitrarily," he admitted. "I look around at what it seems that other people are being paid. To find out, I just ask them. And I ask clients." At the time of the *T&D* interview, this consultant, a management development specialist based in the Seattle area, was charging between $1,500 and $3,000 a day, plus expenses. And he has no shortage of potential clients; he turns down more than twice as much work as he accepts.

One recommendation for setting your fees is to first ask yourself how much money you want to make each year, keeping in mind the extra expenses—for example, insurance and marketing—you'll have to shoulder as an independent. (The management consultant described above decided he wanted to make $160,000 a year.) Next, determine how many billable days a year you want to work. (His choice was eighty days.) Then do the math. (The Seattle-based consultant determined that he had to bring in an average of $2,000 a day in order to meet his goals.)

Remember that those are eighty *billable* days. An independent consultant is a small-business owner. As such, you'll work many hours with no paycheck—especially at first—marketing your services, handling general administrative tasks, and developing your skills and contacts.

Another option for an independent consultant is to contract for work from a large consulting firm. Your fees will be much smaller this way; a career-development specialist in southern California told *T&D* that her fee starts at $300 a day for this kind of work. The advantages of contracting with a larger consulting firm is that you're spared the work of finding clients. It may be a good arrangement to consider, especially if you're just starting out as a consultant. As you build up your own practice, you can gradually cut back on the amount of work you accept from other consulting firms.

WORKING CONDITIONS

What are working conditions like for professionals in the field of training and development? They vary dramatically, depending on the type of work you do, the kind of organization you work for, and your level in your organization. For simplicity, we'll break down our exploration of working conditions in HRD into three sections: in-house practitioners, external consultants, and contract trainers.

In-House Practitioners

Internal training and development specialists are those who are employed within an organization to improve the performance of that organization's own employees and systems. Some—especially in larger companies or agencies—work in departments devoted exclusively to training and development. Others fall under the human resources umbrella and may also have duties involving job classification, recruitment and selection, or personnel administration. Some trainers are subject matter specialists who work for the departments in which they conduct training—for example, engineering, sales and marketing, or information systems.

Like other employees of large- and medium-size firms or government agencies, most in-house training and development professionals who work full-time receive such fringe benefits as health insurance, retirement plans, sick leave, and paid vacation time.

Internal practitioners in training, organization development, and career development have frequent contact with many people inside and outside the organization. Employees at all levels—

from the shop floor to the executive suite—may become work-shop participants or subject matter experts. In-house trainers might also work closely with external training suppliers, union leaders, government representatives, or others from outside of the organization.

Heavy workloads have become a major complaint in today's downsized, streamlined, and reengineered workplaces. The training field is not immune. Most respondents to a fax-in poll of *Training & Development* readers (June 1993) reported feeling overworked either all or most of the time. Most said they work more than ten hours a day, and almost all work on weekends. Those responses might indicate that training specialists work longer hours than other professionals. But the survey was not a scientific study; readers who felt overworked were more likely to fill out the questionnaire. And recent studies show that the average full-time U.S. worker—in any field—puts in forty-seven hours a week. In other words, trainers and HRD specialists work hard, but they can't claim a monopoly on midnight oil. Exact figures are hard to come by, but it seems that trainers and HRD specialists work about as much time as other salaried professionals do—forty to fifty hours a week.

Working conditions for in-house trainers are as varied as the organizations they serve. Much of the work is office or classroom work, with relatively clean, pleasant, and comfortable surroundings. But some trainers, especially technical trainers, conduct training on-site wherever employees work, including factories, hospitals, and military bases. Some trainers have plush private offices and run state-of-the-art corporate universities. Others work in open "bull pen" areas with linoleum floors, metal desks, and cabinets full of flip charts and felt-tip markers. In far-flung organizations, frequent travel may be part of the job, with training and development specialists conducting interventions at branch offices, multiple plants, or suppliers' work sites.

As a training and development professional, you could find yourself in any of the following situations:

- presiding over a high-tech classroom in a corporate training facility
- conducting safety training on the factory floor, wearing overalls and a hard hat
- sitting in your firm's personnel office with an employee who seeks career guidance
- poring over a draft of your new training manual in a cramped cubicle
- poring over a computer screen in a cramped cubicle as you dial up the Internet to ask your trainers' usenet group if anyone has a relevant case study you could include in your new training manual
- pulling up a chair in the executive boardroom to help map out an organizational reengineering effort
- boarding an airplane, laptop computer in hand, to conduct on-site training at your firm's European sales office

In fact, it's not unusual for a training and development professional to fill several of those roles—and countless others—in the same week, or even the same day. That's especially true in small- to medium-size companies, in which a few employees are expected to perform a wide variety of tasks.

An Introduction to Human Resource Development Careers (see Bibliography) cites many rewards and advantages of entering the field. But it also cautions that a career in HRD can be "somewhat risky." That's because in most workplaces, training is considered a staff function rather than a line function. In other words, its contribution to an organization's profits is indirect, unlike that of manufacturing or sales. That can leave training particularly vulnerable to budget cuts and layoffs. In some organizations, HRD specialists perform the difficult job of counseling outplaced workers about career opportunities—only to end up, themselves, as the next employees to need outplacement.

External Consultants

Companies and government agencies that have cut their own training departments' budgets still have to obtain training and development from somebody. That's where external practitioners come in. External training and development consultants practice their craft in virtually all of the environments in which internal practitioners work, and they perform many of the same tasks. The difference, of course, is that they are not employees of those workplaces. That makes for a dramatically different experience.

As an external consultant your workplace will shift as you move from one assignment to another. Predictably consultants tend to travel more than internal practitioners do. You might be in one organization for a few days, weeks, or months before proceeding to the next. You'll deal with a wide variety of people in each of those workplaces, but you'll always deal with them as an outsider. That vantage point can be lonely. It also can provide a unique, objective, and startlingly clear view of an organization's problems and processes. And, as a consultant you can move on to the next challenge before you have time to feel bored or stale in a work situation.

Some consultants work for consulting firms or training suppliers. If you work as an employee of a large consulting company, you'll receive the same kinds of benefits and you'll work the same kinds of hours as employees of any other large firm. When you're working out of your own firm's corporate office rather than a client's site, you'll probably find yourself in pleasant, high-tech surroundings.

At the other end of the spectrum is the one-person consulting firm. As an independent consultant—especially if you're just getting started—you might have to operate out of your basement or spare bedroom. Self-employed consultants buy their own insurance and arrange for their own retirement funds. They may lack easy, inexpensive access to photocopying services, administrative help, and state-of-the-art equipment. On the other hand, they can turn down jobs that don't match their sensibilities or fit their personal goals. Independent consultants also can set their own hours. However, don't expect going solo to open the door to a life of leisure. Many people who escape the corporate life to run their own shows find themselves working more hours than ever before.

As for the level of risk you take in becoming a consultant—well, no job is guaranteed for life (unless you're a Supreme Court Justice). Large training firms are as susceptible to market downturns as are other companies. Independent consultants go out of business all the time. Still, U.S. organizations with 100 or more employees budgeted a whopping $10.3 billion for outside expenditures on training-related products and services in 1995, according to *Training* magazine (October 1995). Those outside expenditures represent 20 percent of total training budgets. The figure is up 4 percent from 1994, indicating that the market for outside services is growing as more organizations outsource training functions. "Employment demand will be particularly strong in management and consulting firms as well as personnel supply firms," predicts the *Occupational Outlook Handbook,* "as businesses increasingly contract out personnel functions or hire personnel specialists on a contractual basis to meet the increasing cost and complexity of training and development programs."

Contract Trainers

Contract training and development work falls somewhere between internal training and external consulting, but the boundaries can be hazy. In fact the IRS reports that many companies mistakenly (and illegally) classify certain internal employees as contract workers.

In general a contract training and development practitioner agrees to an assignment within a company for a specific period of time (usually months or even years) or for the duration of a project, such as the introduction and implementation of a new computer system. Contract trainers work in the same surroundings as their in-house and consulting counterparts. But unlike many consultants (who may be working with several clients simultaneously), they tend to stay in one workplace full-time for an extended period of time. In fact other workers in an organization might not even realize that a particular co-worker is employed on a contract basis. That gives contractors the opportunity to develop close working relationships with in-house colleagues. Unlike an independent consultant, a contract trainer doesn't have to scramble constantly for the next client.

Unfortunately many contract trainers also get stuck with the worst of both worlds. They give up the benefits, organizational support, and relative job security that full-time employees enjoy. They also lack the autonomy and prestige given to an external consultant in the workplace.

PERSONAL MOTIVATIONS

Money, benefits, and working conditions are significant reasons for embarking on a career path and sticking with it. However, other, less tangible factors can be just as important. People choose the training and development field for hundreds of reasons. Some of the more typical ones include personal recognition, advancement, challenging work, opportunities for growth and learning, and a chance to make a difference to an organization or an individual.

Training and development work can be quite visible in an organization. "As an HRD professional, you are likely to gain a high degree of organizational exposure while carrying out your job responsibilities," says *An Introduction to Human Resource Devel-*

opment Careers. That exposure "provides the HRD professional with personal recognition, professional growth, and unique opportunities for advancement in the organization."

The field is challenging and fast moving. Naturally the work requires an understanding of training techniques and principles. It also requires some knowledge of trainees' jobs, whatever they might be. Training professionals have to know about a lot more than just training. Business trends, technology, and systems are always changing; trainers must learn and grow in response to those changes. That gives them the opportunity—and the mandate —to increase their own skills and education in a wide variety of areas. For example, an instructional designer who must develop computer-based courses may first have to learn computer programming or computer-assisted design, adding to his or her own repertoire of skills.

Increasingly management expects training and development specialists to be able to show a connection between the work they do and the company's bottom line. To do so they need a thorough understanding of the organization, its industry, and its basic business tools and tenets. Trainers and organization development specialists who can prove that their efforts have made a difference might be rewarded with raises or bonuses. They'll definitely gain in personal satisfaction.

A different kind of satisfaction comes from working with people and helping them realize their potential. "A love of teaching and presenting" was a factor for 40 percent of *Training & Development* readers who responded to a magazine survey that asked what attracted them to the field (March 1995). Almost as many respondents said they chose the field because they were concerned with the "human side" of work.

"When I was twenty-five, I was diagnosed with Hodgkin's Disease," related respondent Constance MacDonald, now a training consultant in the insurance industry. "The process of confronting my own mortality... made me determined that when I was well enough to return to work, it would be to a job I loved, a job that mattered, a job where I could impact other people's lives."

Almost a third of the readers who answered that survey had an academic background in education. In fact many elementary- and secondary-school teachers get retrained and make the shift to careers in workplace learning; their reasons include higher salaries, greater prestige, and better working conditions.

Another *T&D* survey, reported in December 1994, asked trainers to name the characteristics of a perfect job. The most popular responses to the open-ended question were as follows:

- contact with a wide variety of people
- travel
- flexible hours
- the opportunity to be creative or innovative
- the opportunity to synthesize new information, to learn, and to "stretch"

For some HRD practitioners the most important payback is the chance to contribute to the evolution of the field and of the business world. Industry expert Pat McLagan describes the challenges and opportunities of leading this kind of change. "We must help our organizations focus on the bottom line and on managing and developing people," she writes in the January 1996 issue of *Training & Development.* "Neither can happen without personal development, meaning in work, and a concern for the long-term best interests of the community and environment. HRD practitioners will give voice to these concerns. In fact, HRD may be the only function in a clear position to represent human ethics and morality. . . .

"We could continue to focus mainly on the bottom line and our own professional excellence. But the future seems to require more of us. We must create new ways to address many human resource issues."

CHAPTER 4

EDUCATIONAL REQUIREMENTS AND PREPARATION

SWEEPING CHANGES

Since the 1950s the formal preparation of training professionals has undergone a tidal wave of change. The first response to the demand for workplace education was the "pass-through method." By the 1960s publishers devised specific training packages on a variety of popular workplace topics. Certification programs were designed to train the trainer on the content and methods of these packages.

The 1970s and 1980s saw an increasing demand for identifying a broad range of training competencies. Colleges and universities began offering specific degree and certificate study programs to enhance trainer knowledge and workplace education results.

In the 1990s business productivity is demanding more customized training in every business. At the same time, the application of employee training back on the job must be greatly improved and more clearly measured. This has led to a great expansion in formal undergraduate and graduate programs for training and development.

TRAINING INSTITUTES

How do individuals prepare themselves to become training professionals? Until the 1980s many trainers entered the field through the "back door." Some individuals had been educated in human resources, psychology, or education (elementary/secondary). The vast majority of trainers in the business world were often rotated through the training department as part of their "seasoning" as a business manager. Even today this pass-through method is still a common business practice, particularly in the current era of cost cutting and reengineering.

The pass-through method of trainer education should include several weeks of educational orientation. Many universities have developed training institutes that teach basic instructor behaviors and review content areas such as: adult learning concepts, design, presentation skills, vendor selection, testing, and improving trainer interpersonal skills.

These institute programs seem to be designed mainly for individuals who do not intend to make adult workplace education their career. Presenters of training on a temporary assignment basis general lack the expertise to prepare customized company in-house educational programs. However, they are good candidates to be certified for the standardized training package, which we discuss below.

TRAINING PACKAGE CERTIFICATION PROGRAMS

A wealth of prepared, packaged materials currently exist to meet a variety of training needs. For many training situations there are advantages in utilizing these external resources to assist with solutions to business issues.

One of the key benefits of using training packages is that the research, design, development, and testing, which are both time consuming and costly, already have been performed, and the materials are ready for your immediate use. For additional fees packaged generic programs can be customized for a client. Customization varies from putting a client's logo on printed materials to developing case studies and exercises specific to a client's business or industry. The decision to customize is often determined by the number of participants for which the program is purchased. If the number of employees needing the program is great, then the cost of customizing decreases and becomes a better investment.

Besides tailoring, many program providers offer other services, such as consultation or training in the most effective use of the program. In some content areas there are so many choices available that many training decision makers consider packaged programs as commodities. The decision to purchase a package requires understanding the internal needs of the user company and what the company intends to accomplish by using it.

The most critical feature of packaged training programs is the train-the-trainer component. Companies developing packaged programs may include a train-the-trainer component that provides the client's internal trainers/facilitators with the experience to learn not only the content of the program, but also the most effective methods to use in presenting the program. During this train-the-trainer component, participants actually practice presenting content segments of the program and receive feedback to assist them in improving and further developing their skills. Those who go through the train-the-trainer component are certified as presenters, and only these certified trainers can present the programs to the company's employees.

COMPETENCY MODEL

In the early 1980s, and again in 1989, the American Society for Training and Development (ASTD), the largest professional association in this field, issued a competency model that incorporates thirty-five skill areas that were deemed essential.

A recent survey of Midwest training and development professionals (Kanter 1996) ranked their perceptions of the importance of these skills areas for entry-level trainers (see Figure 4.1). The majority of these competencies were deemed either "extremely important" or "important." Notable exceptions included: understanding career development theories and techniques and using electronic systems (computer-based training, satellite networks, and so forth) to deliver training. A surprisingly large number of these executives also were "indifferent" about a trainer's ability to: plan and coordinate a training program's logistics; use research skills in selecting, developing, or using training; use cost-benefit analysis to assess training alternatives/results; develop management delegation skills; understand the key concepts of their industry; know organization development concepts and strategies; understand their own business's operations, structure, and strategic issues; develop records management skills; or be able to synthesize data and gather information from various reference sources.

Figure 4.1.   Rating the Importance of Selected Competencies as Selection Criteria for Entry-Level Trainers

Rating Scale
(5) Extremely Important (4) Important (3) Indifferent
(2) Unimportant (1) Extremely Unimportant

A. Technical Competencies (Having functional knowledge and skills)					
	Rating				
	5	**4**	**3**	**2**	**1**
1. **Adult Learning Understanding:** Knowing how adults acquire and use knowledge, skills, attitudes; understanding individual differences in learning.	68%	26%	6%	0%	0%

2.	**Career Development Theories and Techniques Understanding:** Knowing the techniques and methods used in career development; understanding their appropriate uses.	8%	31%	49%	12%	0%
3.	**Competency Identification Skills:** Identifying the knowledge and skill requirements of jobs, tasks, and roles.	47%	38%	13%	2%	0%
4.	**Computer Competence:** Understanding and/or using computer applications.	26%	44%	27%	2%	1%
5.	**Electronic Systems Skill:** Having knowledge of function, features, and potential applications of electronic systems for the delivery and management of HRD (such as computer-based training, teleconferencing, expert systems, interactive video, satellite networks).	8%	31%	47%	11%	4%
6.	**Facilities Skill:** Planning and coordinating logistics in an efficient and cost-effective manner.	20%	46%	30%	4%	0%
7.	**Objectives Preparation Skill:** Preparing clear statements that describe desired outputs.	45%	40%	14%	1%	0%
8.	**Performance Observation Skills:** Tracking and describing behaviors and their effects.	38%	42%	15%	4%	1%
9.	**Subject Matter Understanding:** Knowing the content of a given function or discipline being addressed.	40%	38%	18%	5%	0%
10.	**Training and Development Theories and Techniques Understanding:** Knowing the techniques and methods used in training; understanding their appropriate uses.	53%	34%	8%	4%	1%
11.	**Research Skills:** Selecting, developing, and using methodologies, statistical and data collection techniques for a formal inquiry.	8%	53%	28%	11%	0%

Source: ASTD.

B. Business/Management Competencies
(Having a strong management, economics, or administration base)

		Rating			
	5	4	3	2	1
12. **Business Understanding:** Knowing how the functions of a business work and relate to each other; knowing the economic impact of business decisions.	40%	40%	15%	4%	0%
13. **Cost-Benefit Analysis Skill:** Assessing alternatives in terms of their financial, psychological, and strategic advantages and disadvantages.	27%	46%	22%	5%	0%
14. **Delegation Skill:** Assigning task responsibility and authority to others.	14%	40%	37%	6%	2%
15. **Industry Understanding:** Knowing the key concepts and variables such as critical issues, economic vulnerabilities, measurements, distribution channels, inputs, outputs, and information sources that define an industry or sector.	19%	52%	22%	7%	0%
16. **Organization Behavior Understanding:** Seeing organizations as dynamic, political, economic, and social systems that have multiple goals; using this larger perspective as a framework for understanding and influencing events and change.	38%	40%	16%	6%	0%
17. **Organizational Development Theories Techniques Understanding:** Knowing the techniques and methods used in organization development; understanding their appropriate use.	19%	40%	34%	6%	1%
18. **Organization Understanding:** Knowing the strategy, structure, power networks, financial position, and systems of a specific organization.	25%	46%	25%	5%	0%
19. **Project Management Skill:** Planning, organizing, and monitoring work.	46%	38%	14%	2%	0%
20. **Records Management Skill:** Storing data in easily retrievable form.	19%	42%	35%	2%	1%

Source: ASTD

Rating Scale
(5) Extremely Important (4) Important (3) Indifferent
(2) Unimportant (1) Extremely Unimportant

C. Interpersonal Competencies (Having a strong communication base)					
	Rating				
	5	4	3	2	1
21. **Coaching Skill:** Helping individuals recognize and understand personal needs, values, problems, alternatives, and goals.	48%	38%	9%	5%	0%
22. **Feedback Skill:** Communicating information, opinions, observations, and conclusions so that they are understood and can be acted upon.	60%	35%	1%	4%	0%
23. **Group Process Skill:** Influencing groups so that tasks, relationships, and individual needs are addressed.	53%	40%	5%	1%	1%
24. **Negotiation Skill:** Securing win-win agreements while successfully representing a special interest in a decision situation.	28%	52%	14%	5%	1%
25. **Presentation Skill:** Presenting information orally so that an intended purpose is achieved.	85%	12%	4%	0%	0%
26. **Questioning Skill:** Gathering information from and stimulating insight in individuals and groups through the use of interviews, questionnaires, and other probing methods.	58%	32%	8%	2%	0%
27. **Relationship Building Skill:** Establishing relationships and networks across a broad range of people and groups.	52%	41%	5%	2%	0%
28. **Writing Skill:** Preparing written material that follows generally accepted rules of style and form, is appropriate for the audience, is creative, and accomplishes its intended purpose.	55%	41%	4%	0%	0%

Source: ASTD

Rating Scale
(5) Extremely Important (4) Important (3) Indifferent
(2) Unimportant (1) Extremely Unimportant

D. Intellectual Competencies (Having knowledge and skills related to thinking and processing information)	Rating				
	5	4	3	2	1
29. **Data Reduction Skill:** Scanning, synthesizing, and drawing conclusions from data.	21%	51%	27%	0%	0%
30. **Information Search Skill:** Gathering information from printed and other recorded sources; identifying and using information specialists and reference services and aids.	24%	52%	20%	4%	0%
31. **Intellectual Versatility:** Recognizing, exploring, and using a broad range of ideas and practices; thinking logically and creatively without undue influence from personal biases.	54%	40%	5%	1%	0%
32. **Model Building Skill:** Conceptualizing and developing theoretical and practical frameworks that describe complex ideas in understandable, usable ways.	31%	42%	23%	4%	1%
33. **Observing Skill:** Recognizing objectively what is happening in or across situations.	57%	39%	4%	0%	0%
34. **Self-Knowledge:** Knowing one's personal values, needs, interests, style, and competencies and their effects on others.	52%	39%	8%	0%	0%
35. **Visioning Skill:** Projecting trends and visualizing possible and probable futures and their implications.	31%	46%	22%	1%	0%

Source: ASTD

It appears that many companies do not yet require their trainers/ adult educators to consistently perform these tasks. However, the authors predict that over the next decade the realities of an increasingly competitive marketplace will increase the daily practice of these competencies by the majority of all trainers.

The identification of these business and education competencies was due to the growth and increasing sophistication of American business training. These competencies are causing individual trainers to participate in more comprehensive educational programs that will meet their employers' demands. Higher education began developing degree and certificate programs that address professional training "best practices" in a wide variety of ways.

COLLEGE TRAINING
AND DEVELOPMENT PROGRAMS

Beginning in the 1970s, as the demand for adult workplace education grew, it became apparent that better career preparation for training and development professionals would improve regularly offered and custom-designed company education programs. Advances in the fields of psychology, education, and business have spurred on the development of these new degree programs applied to the training arena.

By the early 1990s U.S. higher education (according to ASTD) was offering more than 60 undergraduate degree programs, more than 140 master's programs, and almost 60 Ph.D. (doctoral) programs in human resource development. These programs cover very broad areas of knowledge, sometimes overlap in their content, or are based on opposing philosophical/practical points of view (see Figure 4.2). We will begin our review first with the programs that were developed at the master's degree level, then with

**Figure 4.2. Higher Education Program Range
in Training & Development**

Program Characteristics	Bachelor's Degree (B.A./B.S.)	Master's Degree (M.A./M.B.A.)	Doctorate (Ph.D.)
	1. *Generalist* Business and education course mix.	1. *Education* Education and psychology course mix.	1. *Educational Psychology*
		2. *Continuing Education* Business, education, and psychology course mix.	2. *Business/Human Resources*
		3. *M.B.A.* Business and human resources concentration.	3. *Industrial Organizational Psychology*
		4. *Technical Design* Computer design, computer assisted instruction, course design emphasis.	
		5. *Industrial/Organizational (I/O) Psychology* Assessment, testing, human resource mix.	

those developed at the B.A./B.S. level, and finally with the programs developed at the Ph.D. level.

Master's Degree Programs

Universities have begun offering graduate programs at the master's level. A typical program in adult and corporate instructional management is offered by Loyola University of Chicago. This master's program includes courses in: instructional methods, instructional design, human resource development, computer-assisted instruction, program evaluation, a review of past-current-future best training practices/concepts, program administration, adult learning, and research (see Figure 4.3). Students must also have either at least six months of training and development work experience or appropriate internship experience as part of their degree requirement.

Another approach is to combine the above areas with traditional business management topics. An example of this model is the master's program in continuing education and training management at the College of St. Francis in Joliet, Illinois. In addition to the education/training courses previously mentioned, students are also required to address core business topics such as: management and organizational behavior, marketing theory and applications, applied research, and financial administration and budgeting (see Figure 4.4).

This interdisciplinary approach seems to address often-heard criticism by businesspeople that trainers are just "educators," that they know "little or nothing about the business process of how a company makes a profit." The truth is that training and development professionals are educators and recognize that adults learn in many ways that are different than children or adolescents. But they are also businesspeople. What will be the outcome of a train-

Figure 4.3.   Loyola University (Chicago) Course Descriptions

ADULT AND CORPORATE INSTRUCTIONAL
MANAGEMENT PROGRAM (ACIM)

CURR 380 (Statistics): This course will provide the learners with skills related to various statistical techniques applicable to test results. The learner will be provided with knowledge and practice in interpreting the findings.

CURR 413 (Instructional Methodology): This course will provide the learner with instructional methods as they apply to the adult learner. The learner will demonstrate instructional skills related to the delivery of a presentation.

CURR 440 (Instructional Design): This course will provide the learner with the skills necessary to design and develop a training seminar. Following an accepted design model, the learner will produce a "Design Document" and "Leader's Guide" for a 6-to-8-hour training seminar.

CURR 450 (Human Resource Development): This course will provide the learner with knowledge of the HRD function. Emphasis will be placed on the role of training and development within the organization and, more specifically, within the HRD function.

CURR 491 (Microcomputers in the Agency): The student will master skills and knowledge associated with word processing, database development, spreadsheet development, and data analysis.

CURR 492 (Computer-Assisted Instruction): This course will provide the learner with the skills necessary to design and develop a computer-assisted learning program. Through guided instruction, the learner will design and develop a computer-assisted learning program using an authoring system.

CURR 496 (Program Evaluation): This course will provide the learner with knowledge necessary to conduct evaluations. The learner will conduct an evaluation of a training program in a natural and realistic setting.

ELPS 420 (Philosophy of Training): In this course, the learner will review leading thinkers as related to philosophical aspects of education/training. The course will also provide the learner with knowledge and skills necessary to use logical and reasoned arguments in support of the training function.

ELPS 460 (Program Administration): This course is designed to provide the learner with an overall view of the management of a training function. Topics such as management theory, budgeting, forecasting, appraisal, and evaluation will be discussed.

CEPS 450 (Adult Learning): The learner will become knowledgeable in the theories of adult learning as they applies to the training function. Emphasis will be placed on the adult in the work setting.

Figure 4.4.   St. Francis (Joliet, Illinois) Course Descriptions

71 901   Management and Organizational Behavior
Provides an overview of the management skills and principles used in today's business environment. The students will be introduced to the human side of organizations. This course will offer insights into how behavior science theory and concepts are applicable in a wide range of organizational settings and situations.

71 902   Foundation of Continuing Education and Training
Introduces the student to the historical, social, and political aspects of continuing education and training. It includes delivery systems in formal and informal settings in business and industry, higher education, continuing professional education, governmental and community agencies, community education, religious organizations, gerontology programs, and health care delivery systems.

71 906   Marketing Theory and Applications
Provides an overview of the marketing skills, theories, and principles used in today's corporate environment. This course emphasizes the practical application of marketing to real-world situations in both profit and not-for-profit institutions.

71 912   Adult Learning and Development
Presents adult learning theory as it applies to factors that influence and facilitate adult participation and learning. It examines various theories of physiological, psychological, and social adult development.

71 922   Instructional Design and Testing
Presents methods of developing and delivering education and training materials. It includes establishing objectives, facilitating group communications, understanding styles of adult learning, utilizing educational technology, and assessing learning outcomes.

71 926   Applied Research Methodology
Emphasizes the application of research methods in management. It introduces the basic tools needed to conduct professional research, including an understanding of the survey method. The student will develop skills needed to evaluate the value and validity of research.

71 932   Program Development and Evaluation
Instructs in determining educational program needs, establishing program objectives, designing and scheduling offerings, and establishing procedures for program evaluation. Program planning strategies are addressed for both primary site delivery and distance education such as extensions and telecommunications.

continued

Figure 4.4.   *continued*

71 942   Financial Administration and Budgeting
Reviews the basic language of accounting and finance. This course covers the development and application of accounting and finance techniques to organizational fiscal activities. It emphasizes managerial understanding and application. Course topics include the accounting function, financial planning, budgeting, fund-raising, and grant writing.

71 952   Administration of Continuing Education and Training
Explores the issues and the practice of leadership in continuing education and training. It includes hiring and evaluating staff, collaboration and group communication skills, conflict resolution skills, establishing a mission statement, integrating education and training into organizational goals and long-range planning.

71 992   Internship in Continuing Education and Training
An optional opportunity for students to work in a setting appropriate to their interests for the purpose of gaining practical experience. It may involve placement in an organization or it may involve a project (such as research or evaluation) in the student's own organization. The internship must be taken after the completion of a minimum of 24 credit hours and before completion of the last course. It is not included in the program's required 36 credit hours. Applications to and permission of the academic advisor are required.

ing program if in preparing teams to solve real-world business problems, the company trainer cannot read a balance sheet or understand how the business makes decisions, conducts its marketing, and addresses competitive industry issues? How can a trainer write and conduct realistic training simulations that help employees improve personal problem-solving/decision-making abilities without knowledge of both applied business systems and education theory/practices?

Another option at the master's degree level is to approach training as part of human resources in a business school's M.B.A. program. Here the student receives a strong grounding in business concepts and systems and an overall understanding of human resources/workplace training. However, the lack of an educational component in the areas previously described considerably weakens the future trainer's ability to realistically address adult learning issues in the workplace.

A further way is to approach these issues from an organizational development (OD) perspective. Many postsecondary institutions are now offering OD programs as part of an M.S. or M.B.A. degree. One such program is taught at Benedictine University in Naperville, a suburban community near Chicago. Its intent is to integrate technical and organization development skills and teach students more effective management styles.

These courses seek to offer students knowledge in both the theory and practice of effective management. OD programs are designed to develop skills in organizational change, assessment, team building, and conflict management, among other potential contemporary managerial issues (see Figure 4.5).

A more technical approach to training and development career preparation is a graduate degree in instructional design. The writing of training programs is a potential major career option. One such degree program is the master's program in human performance and training at Governors State University, University Park, Illinois. This program prepares instructional designers to: analyze training/organizational problems and needs; design, develop, and properly implement training materials; and evaluate training materials and programs. Degree requirements for the programs are shown in Figure 4.6.

Larger corporate training departments often retain full-time course designers to write new, customized company courses. (See Chapter 2, Training and Development as an Organization.) The use of computers to aid in the "hard copy" design process of training material is becoming increasingly important. Also, designing computer-based training, or interactive video, and using distance-learning technologies are now an integral part of training design.

**Figure 4.5.   Benedictine University (Naperville, Illinois)
Course Descriptions**

MGMT 580   Group Dynamics
Deals with the dynamics of group and interpersonal relationships. Uses extensive group experience (laboratory
training) to help students become more aware of how their
actions affect and are affected by others, more capable of
giving and receiving personal feedback, and more cognizant
of the dynamic process by which groups are created, main-
tained and transformed. Studies major concepts in group
and interpersonal relations, including communication patterns' influence on power dynamics, conflict management,
interpersonal perception, trust formation, leadership, and
task group dynamics.

MGMT 581   Team Building
Develops a working knowledge of team building, its theoretical basis, and its strengths and weaknesses as an organization development intervention.

MGMT 582   Conflict Management
Explores intrapersonal, interpersonal, and intragroup conflict and conflict management. Examines underlying causes,
participant strategies and outcomes, and effective management strategies. Draws concepts from sociology, psychology, and political sciences, using both cognitive and
affective learning experiences.

MGMT 583   Organizational Assessment
Reviews various means and methods for conducting organizational diagnosis and assessment as organization development interventions.

MGMT 584   Strategies for Change
Reviews the development and implementation of successful
change. Focuses on the development of diagnostic skills and
the selection of appropriate change methods. Includes
exploration of the roles of the change agent, employee
involvement, and political issues.

continued

Figure 4.5.   *continued*

MGMT 585   Quality of Work Life
Covers the development of appropriate levels of employee participation, increasing the psychological rewards of the employee and the quality and productivity of the organization. Emphasizes the design of high-performance work systems for total quality.

MGMT 586   International Organization Development
Examines and analyzes OD values and their relationship with national and cultural values in countries around the world. Consists of an overview and case studies involving application and adaptation of management and OD practices to local situations differing by organizational and national culture.

MGMT 593   Process Consultation
Covers the concepts, methods, and philosophy of process consultation and its role in organization development. Emphasizes the application of this key activity in consulting to organizations, groups, and individuals. Is presented in a context useful to consultants and managers alike.

MGMT 632   Organizational Development
Considers theory and practice of organizational change and organizational development. Discusses analysis, planning, implementation, and evaluation of change programs. Covers the learning process, OD interventions, consultant skills, employee participation, monitoring success, reinforcement, and ethical issues.

A master's level degree in industrial/organizational (I/O) psychology is a narrower career option. Graduates from these programs often find positions in areas of business compensation, data analysis, training, or generalist human resource management.

The educational guidelines suggested by the Society for I/O Psychology, Inc. (a division of the American Psychological Association) for education at the master's level include: the core psychological domains, data collection and analysis skills, core industrial/organizational domains, and additional I/O psychology topics (see Figure 4.7).

The professional aspects of I/O psychology careers include: personnel research, training and development, psychological testing research, counseling and consulting (coaching), advising man-

Figure 4.6.   Governors State University (University Park, Illinois)

DEGREE REQUIREMENTS

Required courses:	22–24 Hours
Introduction to Communications and Training	1
Survey of Research Literature	3
Internship/Project/Thesis	2–4
Training Product Design	3
Computer-Based Training I	3
Training Course Development	3
Training Techniques	3
Consulting and Teamwork in Human Performance & Training (HP&T)	3
Seminar: HP&T in Business and Industry	1
Select 14 credit hours from the following:	
Computer-Based Training II	3
Advanced Interactive Instruction	3
Principles of Message Design	3
Scriptwriting for Instruction and Training	3
Evaluation/Cost-Benefit Analysis in HP&T	3
Solving Performance Problems	3
Project Management in HP&T	3
Performance in Organizations	3
Organizational Communication, Change, and Development	3
Total	36–38 Hours

**Figure 4.7. Guidelines Suggested by the Society
for I/O Psychology, Inc.**

AREAS OF COMPETENCE TO BE DEVELOPED
IN MASTER'S LEVEL I/O PSYCHOLOGY PROGRAMS

This table lists the recommended areas of competence to be developed in students in master's level I/O programs. Competencies listed in section I may be obtained as part of the student's psychological training at the undergraduate level. Competencies listed in section IV are optional.

I.   Core Psychological Domain (may be acquired at the undergraduate level)

    A.   History and Systems of Psychology

    B.   Fields of Psychology

II. Data Collection and Analysis Skills

    A.   Research Methods

    B.   Statistical Methods/Data Analysis

III. Core Industrial/Organizational Domains

    A.   Ethical, Legal, and Professional Contexts

    B.   Measurement of Individual Differences

    C.   Criterion Theory and Development

    D.   Job and Task Analysis

    E.   Employee Selection, Placement, and Classification

    F.   Performance Appraisal and Feedback

    G.   Training: Theory, Program Design, and Evaluation

    H.   Work Motivation

    I.   Attitude Theory

    J.   Small-Group Theory and Process

    K.   Organization Theory

    L.   Organizational Development

IV. Additional Industrial/Organizational Domains (educational experiences in these domains are considered desirable but not essential)

    A.   Career Development Theory

    B.   Human Performance/Human Factors

    C.   Consumer Behavior

    D.   Compensation and Benefits

    E.   Industrial and Labor Relations

Source: Society for Industrial and Organizational Psychology, Inc. (Division of the American Psychological Association)

agement, setting personnel policy, human resource planning, organizational development and analysis, and other human resource functions. It is important to understand that many of these areas can be fully addressed only by the completion of a Ph.D. in I/O psychology. Master's students learn core competencies (for example, regression analysis and classical test theory) but are exposed only to higher level concepts (for example, causal modeling and generalizability theory).

University programs lead to the M.A., M.S., or Ph.D. degree in psychology with a specialization in I/O psychology. A typical master's degree requires two to three years of education. This is equivalent to the other M.A. options previously discussed.

All of these master's programs are currently targeted to individuals who are already in company training departments or who are seeking to change careers. Current trainers may use these graduate studies to prepare for management/supervisory positions or just to broaden skills and update their knowledge.

Bachelor's Degree Programs

Only in the 1990s have colleges and universities begun exploring a bachelor's degree in this field. However, business and education departments have long offered individual courses touching on adult workplace learning. As we have already noted in connection with master's programs, the interdisciplinary nature of the most desirable curriculum has long been a major obstacle to the development of a training major for a bachelor's degree.

The advent of the "corporate university," the "learning organization," and "lifelong learning" concepts have dramatically increased demand for the development of a basic college credential for entry-level positions in corporate training departments and provided legitimate professional standing among the swelling ranks of training consultants. To this end several universities have begun to offer undergraduate programs. The University of Wisconsin (Stout) has developed a specialization in training that is transferable to any business or industry. Another comparable example is the program at the University of Minnesota (St. Paul), also designed at an introductory undergraduate level. By offering these specialized programs, these universities have recognized the interdisciplinary components that are necessary to prepare training professionals. These undergraduate programs offer the promise of greater flexibility in future employment opportunities (see Figure 4.8).

The authors see a growing value to preparing all future workplace adult educators through such core educational programs. For many years the major professional societies in the field—the American Society for Training and Development (ASTD), the International Society for Performance Improvement (ISPI), and the Organizational Development Network (ODN)—have debated instituting certification programs. This has proven to be an impossible task because of the great diversity now found in the ranks of training and development professionals. In the mid-1990s, due to a new flood of training consultants, the legitimacy of the field continued to erode both in the eyes of business management and educators. Agreement is needed on a core knowledge base for training. Without recognized college degree programs there has been little hope of moving adult workplace learning beyond its present largely haphazard application throughout most of U.S. business.

The authors believe that the development of a bachelor's degree major in adult workplace education will ultimately become the entry-level requirement desired by most American companies. It will help the business community to recognize that the application of specific knowledge regarding adult workplace learning can have a major impact on the bottom line.

**Figure 4.8.   Coursework Needed in B.A. Training & Development,
University of Wisconsin (Stout)**

Organizational Leadership

An overview of the supervisor's role in meeting organizational objectives through human resource management, supervisory communication skills, motivation, and initiation of change within organizations.

Human Resource Management

Organization and coordination of personnel practices and methods. Includes orientation and training, working conditions, supervision, performance evaluation, and labor relations.

Task Analysis

Task analysis techniques utilized in curriculum development. Topics include occupational and needs analysis, competency identification, and objective writing. Task analysis assists in developing and revising vocational curriculum or job training.

Psychology of Learning

Principles and theories of learning drawn from experimental and theoretical psychology. Contemporary views of learning theory are emphasized.

Adult Education

Philosophy and history of adult education in the United States. Techniques for teaching adults, psychological factors, methods, adult interests and characteristics. *Or choose any acceptable course that acquaints students with theories and principles of learning.*

Audiovisual Communication

Methods of selecting and using audiovisual materials effectively. Experience in operating microcomputers and audiovisual equipment, producing media, and using basic presentation techniques.

Training Methods in Business and Industry

Identification of situations in which the development and delivery of training is needed. Emphasis on methods to deliver a training session. *Or choose any acceptable course involving the study of contemporary teaching and training methods.*

continued

Figure 4.8.   *continued*

Curriculum Development or Course Construction
>Any acceptable course that covers developing curriculum materials, including content analysis, lesson planning, and course management.

Evaluation Course
>Any acceptable course covering program and course evaluation systems and in which teacher- or instructor-developed tests are emphasized.

Co-op/Internship—Training and Development *or*
Internship in Training and Human Resource Development
>Experience in a training and human resource development department consisting of on-site work.

Doctoral Programs

The Ph.D. for careers in training and development is generally meant for those who seek to teach at the college/university level, at least on a part-time basis, and wish to write for publication on adult workplace education issues.

The most common graduate programs are now found in psychology departments as part of educational psychology or industrial/organizational psychology. The science and profession of educational psychology is the branch of psychology that is concerned with the development, evaluation, and application of the theories and principles of human learning, teaching, and training and development. These theory-driven educational applications can then be successfully used to enhance lifelong learning activities in the workplace.

The Ph.D. program in educational psychology at Loyola University, Chicago, allows students to concentrate on adult workforce education issues. It requires students to demonstrate appropriate application of theory to practice for training and industry. In addition to the required core competency courses in educational psychology (i.e., cognition and instruction, motivation, human development, measurement, and research methods, among others), it offers proficiency in adult workplace learning areas such as literacy and issues in professional training. The Ph.D. in I/O psychology offers students more in-depth study in personnel, performance, and assessment issues as previously discussed in the I/O master's degree programs (see Figure 4.7). The major difference is that this advanced degree enables professionals to pursue a university teaching/research career.

An additional or alternative developmental area includes offering business consulting services. In a recent survey of Ph.D. I/O psychologist members, the American Psychological Association showed that the four major career activities of its members included: education, research grants, instruments (test design and review), and consultation (see Figure 4.9).

NEW CREDENTIALS
FOR THE CORPORATE UNIVERSITY

As we review the variety of educational options at the bachelor's, master's, and doctoral levels, it becomes more apparent that education in the workplace is a very complex strategic issue for every business. The preparation of managers to educate employees deserves the careful use by organizations of degreed professionals for entry-level, mid-range, and advanced managerial career positions.

It is impossible to predict at present whether in implementing "the learning organization" U.S. businesses will predominantly use more or fewer internal or external training professionals. However, one trend seems inescapable. As society demands more and more sophisticated technology and business management systems, business will continue to demand better prepared managers of the corporate education process.

**Figure 4.9. I/O Psychologist—Recent Activities
Relative to Work Functions**

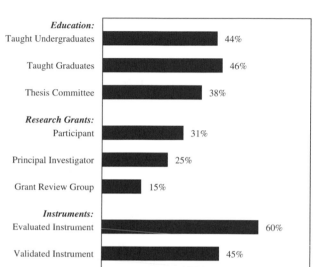

Education:
Taught Undergraduates — 44%
Taught Graduates — 46%
Thesis Committee — 38%

Research Grants:
Participant — 31%
Principal Investigator — 25%
Grant Review Group — 15%

Instruments:
Evaluated Instrument — 60%
Validated Instrument — 45%
Performance Appraisal — 41%
Published Instrument — 7%

Consultation:
Consulted, private organization — 69%
Consulted, government organization — 39%
Consulted outside U.S. — 27%
Expert Witness — 14%

0%   20%   40%   60%   80%

Proportion of Respondents

Source: American Psychological Association

CHAPTER 5

CAREER MANAGEMENT

THE CONTEMPORARY JOB MARKET

One way to understand the job market for training professionals is to divide it into two broad categories: the open, public one and the hidden, unpublished one. A realistic breakdown might be 40 percent open, 60 percent closed. Although these are only our best estimates, the important point is for adult workplace educators to tap into both sides of the employment market.

The published market is readily accessible to you and thousands of other job seekers. Competition is stiff from applicants whose credentials are as good or better than yours. The hidden job market openings occur as the result of: retirement, resignation, promotion, illness, expansion, relocation, mergers, government regulations, and product changes to meet customer demands. Some jobs become public knowledge through the media; many other positions never become widely known.

What are the common reference sources of the hidden job market? To begin with there are the industry magazines or newsletters that exist for just about every business sector in the United States and Canada. Your local public library probably has many of these publications, and college libraries may have many more. Many additional publications are associated with the professional organizations you might consider joining. *The Occupational Outlook*

Handbook, a publication of the U.S. Department of Labor's Bureau of Labor Statistics, and the *Encyclopedia of Associations,* published by Gale Research Inc., are good sources for locating these business organizations. Trade and professional organizations are an excellent source of job leads through their own placement services. (See Chapter 7 on professional information and networking). By becoming active in such organizations and attending their monthly/annual meetings, you find out what is happening in local commerce and industry, meet colleagues with similar interests, and thus begin your personal networking activities.

Networking is important, but it is an activity we must do throughout our careers, not just during a job search. Networking is a lifeline to a profession; it keeps you in touch with reality. Information gathering is the primary goal of informal networking. This involves casual calls to friends and colleagues, attending social and cultural activities, participating in various events, and meeting and talking with people wherever you are. Another networking strategy is the information interview, an informational conversation with a professional to inquire about an industry, company, or job prospect. One of its primary goals is to ask for names of other contacts you might call for additional information.

Ultimately you will discover that people are the best conduit to the hidden job market. You may hear about openings or promotions at an informal gathering or when making an information call to a local trade association office. Developing good interpersonal skills is an essential part of your career development job search.

The primary information sources in the open job market are the classified ads that are run in daily newspapers as well as special interest magazines and newsletters. Ads come from companies, employment agencies, temporary services firms, search firms, and career counseling firms. These classified ads are either real, phoney, or blind. Some companies run ads, not because they have job openings, but because they want to see what the current applicant pool looks like. Blind ads are usually just a practical tactic for reducing paper and phone work. When using classified ads, track a number of publications in addition to your local newspapers.

PREPARING YOUR RESUME

The primary objective of the resume is to present your background and qualifications in a clear and concise way so that potential employers will read it and conclude that you are worth interviewing. Do resumes work? Draw your own conclusions based on these very interesting statistics:

- AT&T and IBM receive more than one million resumes each year
- Johnson & Johnson gets 300,000 resumes a year
- During November through April, the peak recruiting period, many large companies receive an average of 1,000 resumes a week
- Apple Computer and Sun Microsystems get close to 3,000 resumes a week

With so many resumes circulating, you might wonder what happens to them. Human resource folks admit to: "spending 30 seconds reviewing a resume," "skimming every 10th one," "trashing a resume if it doesn't grab my attention in 15 seconds," "using resume-scanning software." Are there alternatives to a good resume? One method supported by many successful job applicants is to:

1. Research companies you want to work for.
2. Find a person or intermediary who actually does the hiring or who is one of the decision makers.
3. Send a combined letter-resume.

A letter-resume is a personal marketing tool. You are the product, and you are selling yourself in a customized letter. Your opening statement should not be an idle comment or a flip promise. State how you heard about a job—through contacts or by some creative snooping! Get to the point. Concentrate on jobs you had that sell you the best and relate to the job in which you are interested. Brevity is crucial. In place of a conventional closing, state a specific follow-up time and date; then be sure to call on that day. When you are satisfied with your letter, check your spelling, grammar, and punctuation. Don't send the letter immediately. Set it aside for a few hours or overnight and then come back to it, making revisions as needed.

Your letter-resume should tailor your experience to the employer's needs, be brief and focused, present facts and figures to document your accomplishments, and be addressed to a specific person.

INTERVIEWING SKILLS

Think of an interview as a professional dialogue, a conversation, for which you are well prepared. Knowing about the company you are interested in helps you determine what aspects of your professional background the employer will value most. Remember that first impressions count. Employers consistently rate these issues as most important:

- arrive on time
- wear a neat, appropriate outfit
- provide an easy-to-read, up-to-date resume tailored to the position

After the interview, follow through with a phone call and a personal thank you note. These strategies will help maintain your competitive edge after an interview. The interviewing process provides an opportunity to meet people in your field, learn about different companies, and build confidence. Interviewing is a learning opportunity that takes time. Thinking of the interview in this broader sense will make it a positive experience. It will also ultimately lead you to the job you need and develop the career you want.

OCCUPATIONAL OUTLOOK/
THE IRRESISTIBLE MOVE TOWARD TECHNOLOGY

How will training professionals be employed as most U.S. businesses implement "the learning organization"? From 1980 to the mid-1990s corporate training departments have resembled a phoenix rising from its ashes, only to dissolve once again. The 1980s witnessed a steady growth in the number and diversity of professionals employed inside training departments. Starting salaries grew. Then the advent of business process reengineering reversed this trend. Companies began shedding trainers and transferring these functions to interim professionals.

Unlike the training consultants of the past, these interim employees are hired for a specific job, and then they are let go. Building an ongoing consulting relationship is not deemed very important. Businesses seek a precise fit of skills/knowledge to the training assignment, and the trend is for rapid "just-in-time training." Trainers must already know the content material and be up-to-date on the design options that make the most sense for a specific audience.

Continuing professional education will be the only means of survival for trainers, even after completing a master's or doctoral degree program. Why? Because ongoing, fundamental, high-tech change is driving the career process ever faster.

What types of adult training professionals will be needed in the workplace? Two trends are now emerging that seem to indicate important areas of growth: computers and critical thinking. High-tech computers and robotics are now creating a business revolution not about quality or flexibility, but about information. More and more powerful computers are linking matter and information. Future trainers will have a very compelling need to learn and understand a variety of business computer applications, such as computer-aided design (CAD). The Boeing 777 was the world's first commercial aircraft largely configured using CAD. CAD will become pervasive not just in manufacturing but throughout business. Workforce educators will need to master computer applications and how they can be applied to numerous business situations. As technology transforms shop floors, offices, and service areas, the workforce will require training in new sets of skills. But computers and robots cannot think. People need to be trained how to develop their critical thinking abilities to produce and use these technological innovations. Teaching critical-thinking strategies will become the second career opportunity for many trainers.

As the twenty-first century unfolds, organizations will require fewer workers, but those who remain must be able to perform at higher cognitive levels. Cognitive-based, critical-thinking skills will be needed by everyone in a business to better manipulate and understand information that leads to various business innovations.

What all this means to future workforce educators is that they will play a pivotal role in teaching these critical skills. CAD and other future technologies will be of little value unless the people using them can analyze, contrast and compare, and use combinational logic to determine a myriad of potential solutions and rank each one's applicability to a given situation. An adult trainer's personal occupational outlook will rest on an ability to enhance employee human potential to evolve, to create, to act on, and to process new information.

The high-tech nature of the twenty-first century and training in critical thinking have the potential of freeing the majority of workers from grunt labor. This is the future of careers in training.

It is exciting and it involves everyone—with trainers performing an essential function.

CAREER EXPECTATIONS

Over the past thirty years and into the next millennium, American business has undergone, and will undergo, a fundamental change in the concept of the manager (see Figure 5.1). In the 1960s industry used traditional behavioral methods to teach skills to managers. Training was seen as a "technique, packages of behavioral techniques, gimmicks." Far too often complex management skills were reduced to a "ten-step process." Senior management vision was conferred downward and throughout the organization. Rewards were based upon how well individual managers followed this corporate culture driven from the top. Few mavericks or creative types were encouraged or tolerated.

The introduction of computers began to shift the emphasis to training groups of managers (department heads) in a systems approach that broadened their business knowledge. Organizational development for senior management was seen as a strategic tool to further this process at the top levels of business.

By the 1980s the new technologies were beginning to bypass middle-management and place daily decisions into the hands of first-line supervisors and even shop foreman or service supervisors. Often middle management became redundant, leading to much corporate downsizing. International competition was beginning to offer consumers far more product and service choices. Shorter, more diverse product runs and innovative service solutions began requiring, for the first time, that supervisors be trained to develop new approaches. Quality circles began to involve employees in the management development process. These programs were an additional response to the high-tech business pressures.

Figure 5.1. Time Line of Management Development Trends (1960–2020)

Audiences	Train Skills	Broaden Knowledge	Develop New Approaches/Teams	Create Fundamental Change/Empower Thinking
Employee-Empowered Work Teams				World Competitive Practices
Supervisors/Quality Circles				
Department Managers and Organizational Development (OD)				
Individual Managers	Traditional Behavioral "Training by Technique"			
	1960s	1970s	1980s	1990–2020

89

MANAGEMENT DEVELOPMENT TRENDS

In the 1990s and well into the twenty-first century, world competitive business practices will require all organizations to do more with less. American business is fundamentally changing the way it manages itself in order to survive and prosper. Employee-empowered work teams are being trained across America to solve problems, think, and create new ideas. We predict that the artificial divisions between management and employees will continue to blur. Team leaders are needed to give direction, monitor, and challenge, but not wield, iron control.

The new organizational structure is flatter, with cooperation replacing fiefdoms and day-to-day business responsibility pushed down and throughout the organization. Traditional methods of evaluation and promotion are being replaced by compensation based on supporting the team's performance. For a company to gain a true competitive edge in the future, business decisions to develop the team's work abilities must come ahead of the quarterly bottom line.

This raises a large number of training issues as more and more managers, professionals, and technicians begin discovering their rapid technical obsolescence, even if they have had very advanced training. Estimates are that the engineer's education has a half-life of five years, meaning that half of what is learned in school is obsolete five years after graduation.

Other issues are driving American business toward far better employee education programs. The link between school and work needs to be established through direct business collaboration with colleges and secondary schools to prepare youth for new, emerging occupations. Severe shortages of skilled technical workers have begun, and will increase, unless American business adapts education models pioneered by European industry.

We need to better inform the public that high-skilled, high-tech jobs are highly paid jobs. When will American society begin to realize that the future of work means fewer and fewer managers and more and more skilled technicians?

At present too many college marketing, finance, and communications graduates are selling neckties in department stores. Our society has done a terrible job of disseminating high-tech career information to students and parents. We fail to offer America's youth a wider variety of successful adult role models other than those requiring a four-year college degree. Business must lead the charge to change society's attitudes regarding job models and success, or we will continue to experience significant skilled technical job shortages.

Globalization of the economy is encouraging more organizations to compete internationally. In 1991 the United States was the world's largest exporter, selling a record $422 billion in goods and $145 billion in services abroad. Each billion dollars of exported merchandise generates 20,000 jobs. One-third of America's economic growth in the past five years flowed from this surge in foreign sales. About 100,000 U.S. companies do business overseas, including 25,000 with foreign affiliates and 3,500 major multinational companies. One-third of U.S. corporate profits is derived from international business, along with one-sixth of America's jobs. A survey by Ernst & Young in 1993 saw a further globalization of American companies. Most indicated that their most significant market growth will take place outside the United States, in developing countries.

From a corporate education standpoint this means that managers must learn to effectively select, train, and motivate a multicultural workforce. They must be able to communicate in different languages, "read" different cultures accurately, and work with and manage multicultural teams. There is no quicker, better road to follow for internationalizing American managers than the education one. Future training professionals must be able to support these changes at work to meet the new international needs of American business.

CHAPTER 6

NEW PARADIGMS
IN TRAINING & DEVELOPMENT

What does the future hold for specialists in the field of training and development? The jury is still out, but one thing everyone seems to agree on is that workplace learning and organizational development are in transition.

"We think the field is at the mature end of its life cycle and that some outcomes are predictable," say Stan Davis and Jim Botkin in the May 1994 issue of *Training & Development.* "Mature industries tend to consolidate; expect this to happen to the training field. . . . Very mature—a euphemism for declining—industries are generally supplanted by a new way of doing things." The consolidation and the creation of new ways of doing things, say Davis and Botkin, "will result in career and business opportunities related to learning that are both monstrously large as well as potentially frightening."

Where will the opportunities lie? Again, it's hard to say. But several trends in training and development have been gaining momentum in recent years.

TOTAL QUALITY MANAGEMENT

Many businesspeople think of the quality movement as something that sprang up, full-blown, in the 1980s. In reality, the roots of total quality management, often called TQM, stretch back to the post–World War II era. That's when American experts W. Edwards Deming and Joseph M. Juran began working with Japanese companies to spread the word about quality improvement—a message that American organizations weren't yet ready to hear.

In the 1970s and early 1980s U.S. companies began their own versions of the "quality circles" that had been so successful in Japanese firms. Quality circles were teams of employees who met to address quality improvement in limited areas of an organization. The circles never really caught on in the United States, mainly because most companies grafted them onto archaic organizational systems that didn't support them—in other words, they weren't part of an integrated approach to quality improvement.

In the 1980s those early forays grew into total quality management, a systematic effort to continuously improve the quality of organizational products and processes. TQM involves "soft" elements such as the development of an organizational culture that values excellence. At the same time it emphasizes the use of hard data to measure quality. Employees tend to work in teams to make improvements, and customer satisfaction is integral to TQM efforts. "Continuous improvement" is a key concept of TQM; in fact, many organizations use the two terms synonymously.

TQM Comes of Age

In 1987 TQM received a seal of approval from the U.S. government, when the Commerce Department instituted the Malcolm Baldrige National Quality Award. The award is administered by the National Institute of Standards and Technology. The Baldrige competition has categories for organizations of various sizes and in all sectors. The award criteria are "continuously improved" from year to year, but they tend to include such categories as leadership, strategic quality planning, information and analysis, and human resource utilization.

The Baldrige selection process includes exhaustive compilation and examination of quality-related records. Applicants for the award receive detailed critiques from the Baldrige examiners. The critiques can be a helpful benchmark for companies trying to board the quality bandwagon. In fact many corporate officials know their firms can't win, but apply for the award simply to receive an evaluation of their TQM progress and suggestions for further efforts.

On the surface it might seem that interest in quality improvement has waned in the mid-1990s. The media attention of a few years ago has dwindled to the occasional profile of a Baldrige winner or mention of the quality-oriented culture at the latest in-vogue firm. But quality hasn't disappeared from the U.S. business landscape; it's simply faded from center stage to become part of the scenery. In an extensive 1995 study by *Training* magazine (October 1995), 58 percent of the 982 responding firms said they have TQM initiatives in place. According to that survey, TQM is particularly prevalent in the manufacturing sector and in the public sector.

The Role of Workplace Learning Professionals

Because the scope of TQM is organization wide, the impetus for successful quality efforts almost always comes from the executive level. But once the decision has been made to pursue total quality, the training department has a major role to play. TQM relies on extensive training, usually for teams of employees. Employees need training in the fundamentals of TQM and in the use of statistical tools for measuring and tracking it. If employees aren't experienced in working on teams, they'll also need training in how to contribute as a team member or leader. Problem-solving skills, decision-making skills, negotiation tactics, diversity management, and interpersonal relations may also be on the training agenda. If TQM is part of a major shift in organizational values, employees will need to know what's expected under the new paradigm. TQM is likely to bring changes to such organizational institutions as performance appraisals, new-employee orientation, and compensation systems. Employees and their managers will need training in the new processes and procedures that result.

Who does all this training? It depends. The training can be designed and delivered by in-house training or HR specialists, by line managers, by a dedicated quality department, or by consultants or contract trainers. Often a company buys packaged or customized training in TQM and trains its in-house trainers to deliver the instruction to employees. A *Training* magazine poll also examined the types of training organizations offer their employees. Of the 821 respondents who answered the question, 58 percent said their organizations provide quality improvement training—and that doesn't even include the teamwork skills, negotiation techniques, and other types of training that may be vital to TQM success. As for the sources of quality-improvement training:

- 13 percent of respondents said they provide quality-improvement training that is designed and delivered exclusively by in-house staff,
- 7 percent of respondents said they use outside providers for TQM training, and
- 39 percent said they use a combination of internal and external providers for quality-improvement training.

No matter which scenario is chosen, training specialists in the area of TQM are likely to have their hands full.

THE LEARNING ORGANIZATION

In an information economy, an organization's success or failure depends on its ability to adapt, change, and innovate; in other words, on its ability to *learn.* "Most competitive improvements can't be bought. They have to be learned," explains Anthony

Patrick Carnevale in the February 1992 issue of *Training & Development.* "In fact, economists estimate that 60 percent of competitive improvements come from learning to make better use of the resources we buy."

That learning must take place continuously, as part of everything an organization does. And it must take place on three levels: the individual level, the team level, and the corporate level.

Peter Senge's book, *The Fifth Discipline,* has become the bible for this new paradigm in workplace learning. In it he describes learning organizations as those "where people continually expand their capacity to create the results they truly desire, where new and expansive patterns of thinking are nurtured, where collective aspiration is set free, and where people are continually learning how to learn together." (For a blueprint of a learning organization, see Figure 8.1.)

Senge describes five disciplines of the learning organization:

- *Personal mastery* is the continuous development of proficiency in what we do, achieved through a commitment to lifelong learning. Senge calls it "the learning organization's spiritual foundation."

- *Mental models* are the personal assumptions and generalizations that influence our behavior, the filters through which we view the world and draw conclusions.

- *Shared vision* is the center around which a learning organization revolves—a common array of goals, values, and missions that people throughout the organization are committed to.

- *Team learning* is a way of leveraging the power of groups. "Teams, not individuals, are the fundamental learning unit in modern organizations," says Senge. "Unless teams can learn, the organization cannot learn."

- *Systems thinking* is Senge's fifth discipline, the one that ties the others together. It is a conceptual framework that looks at seemingly isolated events in the context of connections and implications. It is a focus on both the forest and the trees.

Of course, it's all well and good to provide abstract definitions and characteristics for learning organizations. What about tangible examples? Gordon, Morgan, and Ponticell's book, *Future-Work: The Revolution Reshaping American Business* offers tangible case studies of organizations that are teaching critical thinking skills to their employees at all levels. *FutureWork* also demythologizes Senge's book into understandable business examples of using cognitive-based training rather than behavior-based training to teach employees the skills of problem solving and decision making and how to use them. The Workforce Education Triad (see Chapter 1, Figure 1.3) of skills, training, and education gives business a tangible paradigm around which to organize life-long em-ployee learning in support of a high performance organization.

What Happens to Training
in a Learning Organization?

Where is training's niche in a learning organization? In the May 1994 issue of *Training & Development*, Harvard Business School's Rosabeth Moss Kanter says that workplaces are placing more emphasis on learning—but not necessarily on training. "Training signifies a one-way transfer of established wisdom or skill from the trainer to the unformed trainee," she explains. "It focuses on the teacher, not the student. But learning...involves not only absorbing existing information, but also creating new solutions to not-yet-fully-understood problems. And while we could not conceive of training without students, learning can take place in the absence of teachers."

In a true learning organization, she says, "the ultimate act of learning will be embedded in the person and team as they do their work." As workplace learning is taken out of the classroom and integrated into people's jobs, training becomes less of a separate event. Already most experts note an increase in the number of line managers taking on the responsibility for training their staffs. More training is taking place in self-directed "learning lab" sessions. Also, new technology makes it possible for employees to receive "just-in-time" training on the job—for instance, by calling up help screens on their computers to answer specific questions or demonstrate specific procedures exactly when that help is needed.

Traditionally we've associated workplace learning with the metaphor of the schoolroom. For the learning organization, Senge replaces that metaphor with a new one—the metaphor of the rehearsal hall, where groups work together to produce results and enhance their capacity for success.

What of trainers? What role will training and development specialists play in helping their organizations reach that destination? At first glance it may appear that trainers are being pushed out. If learning is infused into everything employees do, it seems that managers, rather than trainers, will have to take the lead. Couldn't that decentralize training to the extent that trainers would be unnecessary?

Not necessarily, say many experts. Organizations will still need training and development professionals, but only if those people are willing to take on new roles and responsibilities, and only if they are willing to develop new ways of thinking about work, training, and education—in other words, new mental models.

In a May 1994 *Training & Development* magazine article, Senge describes two roles for training and development professionals in a learning organization. First, he says, trainers have the skills and experience to work with managers to plan and facilitate learning. For instance, trainers can help managers or subject-matter experts design and develop lessons for use in computerized learning labs. The other role involves what Senge describes as "guiding the diffusion of new learnings." Line managers may be responsible for making sure that employees learn what they're supposed to learn. However, people who specialize in workplace training and education are in a better position to help employees build on new insights and accomplishments. The key to it all, says Senge, is partnerships between trainers and line managers.

Margaret Wheatley, the author of *Leadership and the New Science,* writes in the same issue of *Training & Development* about trainers' roles in the learning organizations of the future. "Those of us already engaged in training and organizational learning will be challenged to design learning experiences that themselves are not rigidly structured or confined by classroom boundaries. All learning, like most work, will be just-in-time. Long-range planning of courses ... will give way to learning that is available in a variety of forms, all of which are flexible, easy to access, and available wherever needed. The demands for new knowledge and skills will be constant, no longer a value-added element, but the essential factor in determining organizational survival."

Robert Brinkerhoff and Stephen Gill describe a new paradigm for organizational learning in their book, *The Learning Alliance: Systems Thinking in Human Resource Development.* They say that HRD professionals can help build an infrastructure for organizational learning by creating alliances between learners and managers, between the training department and other departments, and among all of an organization's people and processes. They describe four keys to creating those alliances:

- linking training to business needs and strategic goals
- maintaining a strong customer focus in the design, development, and implementation of all training activities
- managing training with a systems view of performance in the organization
- measuring the training process in order to continue improving it

"Whatever training leaders do, they should not become defensive about their role and their contribution to the business," Gill advises in a *Training & Development* article (May 1995) based on the book. "The accumulated learning of all employees is as important to an organization as its property, inventory, equipment and machines, and products and services. It is as important as the loyalty of employees and customers. Training leaders can help companies maximize the value of learning, but first they must examine their own mental models and make the paradigm shift."

THE HIGH-PERFORMANCE WORKPLACE

Closely tied to both the learning organization concept and the TQM movement is the so-called performance paradigm. The restructuring, reengineering, and reinventing of U.S. organizations in the early 1990s left many of us scratching our heads and wondering "What happens next?" For many corporations, nonprofit organizations, and government entities, "what's next" is the high-performance workplace.

How does the performance paradigm differ from the learning organization and total quality management? Actually, all three could work together. The characteristics of the high-performance workplace are compatible with—and enhanced by—those of the learning organization. And TQM can be an effective tool for performance support.

In some ways performance improvement is replacing quality improvement as *the* business trend of the 1990s. Companies that were extolling quality five years ago aren't even using the "Q-word" today. Instead they're raving about performance improvement, performance enhancement, performance support, or high-performance systems. The substitution of performance for quality has led cynics to wonder if the trend makers have simply written a new set of lyrics to the same old song. In some organizations that's a valid concern, but companies that really embrace the performance paradigm are learning a whole new repertoire.

TQM is systemic but adds its own tools and procedures to existing organizational systems; high performance may rethink everything. TQM *affects* all systems in an organization; high performance *involves* all systems. TQM uses a specific set of statistical tools to improve and track performance in small, selected areas; high performance involves an interrelated array of practices, strategies, and procedures for enhancing performance in all parts of the organization.

It's difficult to define a high-performance workplace. High-performance systems are as different as the organizations that develop and implement them. But there are some common traits, says Patricia Galagan in a December 1994 *Training & Development* article. Work is done by customer-focused teams. Employees have skills in many different areas. The organization is actively engaged in managing change. Collaboration is the norm. And technology is crucial to employees' work.

Galagan interviews economist and author Anthony Carnevale, who lists four prerequisites for high performance:

- new, flexible technologies
- new high-performance organizational formats
- a highly skilled and autonomous workforce
- collaborative labor/management relations

Electronic Performance-Support Systems

The new, flexible technologies of the high-performance workplace are of special interest to trainers. These technologies include electronic performance-support systems, also known as EPSSs. A true EPSS is more than a higher-tech system of help screens. It's interactive and just-in-time. It mimics the look and feel of an employee's actual work tasks—or it guides the employee through an actual work task, asking questions that help the employee not only to solve the immediate problem, but to learn how to solve similar problems in the future. EPSSs let learners control not only when they will learn, but how they will learn.

At the moment, experts admit, most so-called EPSSs are merely automated training manuals. But the technology exists to include hypertext links to databases of expert information, to make interfaces more interactive, and to integrate EPSSs more fully into many kinds of work tasks. Training designers must work in partnership with organizational leaders, subject-matter experts, and technical specialists to develop EPSSs that are intelligent, adaptive, and effective job aids.

Training Versus Performance Support

So, your workplace is steering a course toward high performance. How does that change your job as a trainer? Rosabeth Moss Kanter believes the changes will be dramatic. As she writes in the May 1994 issue of *Training & Development,* "The dawning awareness that high-performance work systems, with an emphasis on learning, hold the key to future competitive success represents a tremendous opportunity for the training profession—but only if the profession reinvents itself."

It may seem that performance support is the job of all trainers, but traditionally it has not been—at least not in many organizations. Under the old paradigm, a trainer's job was to develop and deliver training. Under the new paradigm, the job is to improve performance at the individual and organizational levels. Your job title is likely to change. Instead of *trainer,* you might be known as *performance-improvement specialist* or *performance technologist.* But you'll be changing more than your title. If you're to succeed in your new role, you'll need to change your entire way of looking at your work and the way it fits into the organization.

Performance improvement doesn't eschew training. But training is only one tool in the performance technologist's toolbox.

Others include job aids, electronic performance-support systems, and new organizational policies and procedures.

Here's a popular metaphor to explain the difference between training and performance support. You're an employee who is repeatedly late to work because your car blows a tire several times a week. If you call in a trainer, you'll get a helpful and appreciated course in how to change a flat tire—and a requisition for a good spare. Your problem is solved. Well, sort of. You still get flat tires, but now you know how to cope with them.

Now try something different. Instead of a trainer, dial up a performance technologist. The performance technologist doesn't jump at the quickest fix. Instead he or she questions you about all aspects of the problem, even riding to work with you several times. The performance technologist notices that you pass a construction site every morning, where nails are scattered in the street. The performance technologist maps out a new route to work, one that bypasses the construction site. *Voilà!* You never have another flat tire. Periodically, he or she will check to see that you're still flat-free—just in case another construction job should spring up along your new route.

Now let's look at a real-world example. In a traditional organization, management might say to a trainer, "Customers are complaining about our service. Give us a training program to teach the customer-service reps how to be nice to people on the phone." The trainer would develop a program on that topic—or buy a packaged one—and train the employees. At the end of the course, the trainees might have to take a test to prove that they learned what they were supposed to. In addition, the trainer probably asked them to fill out a questionnaire saying whether they liked the training and thought it had helped them.

Under the performance paradigm, the job isn't to deliver training. It's to improve performance. In a high-performance organization, management says to the performance-improvement specialist, "Customers are complaining about our service. Help us determine what the problem is so we can work together to solve it." The performance-improvement specialist, often called a performance technologist, would study the situation and collect statistical and anecdotal information to analyze it. If the source of the problem is lousy telephone skills, perhaps he or she would recommend a training program like the one described above. However, the problem might be unrelated to employee skills. For example, customers could be irked about slow response time. Analysis might show that response time is slow because of corporate structures and procedures that require customer-service reps to obtain approvals from managers up the chain of command before they can take action to solve a customer's problem.

Once the source of the problem is identified, the performance technologist can work with management to come up with solutions that may or may not involve training. Results are measured and tracked in both subjective and objective ways. Has the number of customer complaints decreased? Are they still complaining about the same thing? Have sales improved? What's happened to the rate of turnover among customer-service reps?

As trainers retrain themselves to take on new roles in high-performance organizations, they'll have to expand their knowledge. They'll need to know more about the business climate in which their firms operate, more about the strategic directions of the organization, and more about the business structures and language that are second nature to business leaders. They'll have to be more willing to work as partners with line managers, customers, and subject-matter experts.

Organization Development
for High Performance

We've talked extensively about the way training changes under the performance paradigm. High-performance work systems also require different skills and approaches from organization-development specialists. Companies are under the tremendous pressure to improve their performance. Many are trying to do it by developing new organizational structures that support the push for performance. That includes team-based structures and flatter organizational charts. But the possibilities are endless. Organization developers will have to expand their mental models to think in new ways about how organizations are set up.

Change-management specialists have traditionally used a model that involves setting a goal and methodically charting a path toward it. That doesn't work anymore. The business environment is moving too fast. Keeping up with—and anticipating—external change is an integral component of high performance. Besides, it's difficult to chart a methodical path toward a goal that's always moving.

"What we know about organization change is becoming insufficient," says W. Warner Burke of Columbia University, as quoted in Galagan's article. "We need to know far more about such areas as how to maintain the momentum of change, how to help people deal with the chaos they experience during a transition, and how much and when to communicate about change."

TEAM BUILDING

Team building has long been a subject for workplace training initiatives, but in the past few years its importance has ballooned. More organizations expect employees at all levels and in all areas to work on teams. Teamwork is an integral component of popular business initiatives such as total quality management. It's increasingly important as organizations downsize—leaving fewer employees, who must be able to handle a wider variety of tasks, and fewer middle managers to handle administrative functions such as hiring employees, structuring work, ordering supplies, and evaluating employee performance.

Teams are prevalent in today's business climate. In *Training* magazine's recent survey, reported in its October 1995 issue, 78 percent of responding organizations said that at least some employees work on teams. And 31 percent have at least one team that is classified as "self-directed," meaning it operates with little direction from a direct supervisor. Members of self-directed teams set work schedules, deal directly with customers, arrange for training, deal with suppliers, set performance targets, and handle other tasks usually reserved for managers.

Training for Teamwork

How does the trend toward teamwork affect the jobs of trainers? In the *Training* survey, 70 percent of responding organizations were providing their employees with training in team building. Respondents also named the sources of their team-building training. In 17 percent of the organizations it was designed and delivered by in-house staff only. In 8 percent all team training came from outside sources. And 45 percent of the respondents provide team training through a combination of internal and external sources.

In addition to specific skills for teams, working as part of a team requires a wide array of competencies that many solo employees simply have not developed. Managers—or team members themselves, if a team operates autonomously—might call on trainers for help in many areas, including the following:

- leadership training
- train-the-trainer programs (to teach teammates how to train each other)
- listening skills
- presentation skills
- techniques for conducting meetings

- negotiation tactics
- problem-solving skills
- decision-making skills

WORKFORCE DIVERSITY

The diversity of the U.S. workforce has become a business issue in recent years. If demographic and societal trends continue as predicted, it will be even more of an issue as we move into the twenty-first century. That means that workplaces are beginning to embrace diversity programs as more than a way to stay out of lawsuits or as "a nice thing to do." Learning to manage diverse workers and to make full use of a wide variety of talents and backgrounds has become a business imperative. Nowhere is this more important than among employees who must work closely as a team.

Women make up roughly half of a workforce that was once predominantly male. The Americans with Disabilities Act is opening corporate doors to workers with a wide variety of physical and mental disabilities. More U.S. workers belong to minority ethnic or national groups. Immigration is up. More employees who are gay, lesbian, and bisexual are refusing to hide their identities. And most large firms are now doing business internationally, which means that employees from around the world might be part of the same work team.

What does this mean for teams and for the people who train them to work as teams? The *Training* magazine poll showed diversity as a training topic in 53 percent of the organizations surveyed. Diversity training can be tricky because it addresses issues that can be controversial and highly personal. It should focus on behaviors in the workplace—not on beliefs. It should emphasize the contributions of all employees—including white men. Most important it should be handled only by a practitioner with solid experience in diversity efforts. For that reason many companies choose to bring in consultants with diversity expertise. A bad diversity program can be worse than no program at all, and the result can be disastrous for diverse team members who are trying to forge ways of working together.

EXPERIENTIAL AND ADVENTURE LEARNING

Experiential learning, or learning by doing, makes use of a basic learning principle: People learn more when they are actively engaged in the learning process. Experiential learning can involve role plays and simulations, "game show" activities, and team problem-solving exercises. But the term is closely associated with a particularly high-profile type of experiential learning. It's called adventure learning, and it often takes place outdoors, away from the workplace. Members of a work team go through a program together in order to build teamwork skills and camaraderie.

Proponents of adventure learning say it helps teams find new ways of working together to achieve goals, promotes trust among teammates, sparks creativity, and provides a common language and shared metaphors that can be applied later at work.

Adventure learning comes in three basic varieties:

- *Wilderness programs* usually involve an outdoor activity such as white-water rafting, mountain climbing, or sailing. Participants live outdoors or in rustic accommodations for the duration.
- *High-impact programs* include activities that take place well above the ground. Trainees might climb around on high-ropes courses, walk a balance beam high up in the trees, or scale a high wall.

• *Low-impact programs* rarely go above eye level. For instance, trainees might work on a low-ropes course or lead each other around on blindfolded "trust" walks. Some low-impact activities can take place indoors.

Each kind of learning has its advantages and drawbacks. A high degree of risk (or perceived risk) can enhance learning by forcing participants to engage themselves more actively in the exercises and by providing a more dramatic emotional experience. But some high-risk programs could be impossible for employees who are less than athletic. Low-impact programs that can be held inside have the advantage of being unaffected by the vagaries of the weather. A major drawback to wilderness programs is that they tend to be extremely expensive, costing thousands of dollars per participant.

Not surprisingly, outdoor experiential programs are quite controversial, especially those that are seen as an excuse for executives to take a wilderness vacation on the company's time. In fact some organizations contribute to that perception by using the programs as perks for corporate leaders or rewards for top performers. Legal liabilities are also a potential pitfall, especially with the higher-risk exercises and those that might not offer equal access to employees of all levels of physical ability.

Because of the risks involved and the specialized facilities needed for most outdoor experiential programs, virtually all of this type of training is outsourced. Corporations contract with firms that specialize in adventure-based activities, and facilitators include workplace learning specialists as well as experts in the more physical aspects of the programs. Trainers who are charged with contracting for such services must be sure to check out the level of physical risk and the suitability of the planned activities for the targeted employees.

It's also crucial to ask questions about how the facilitators plan to follow up the physical activities. The further removed an exercise is from the reality of the workplace, the more important it is to debrief teammates afterwards in order to reinforce the learning and make the connections to the team's real work crystal clear.

DISTANCE LEARNING

When Thomas Campbell wrote "distance lends enchantment" in 1799, he could have been predicting training delivery methods of the 1990s and beyond. Today large corporations and government agencies are beginning to discover some enchanting possibilities in distance-learning technologies.

Many trainers and organizational leaders see distance learning as the wave of the future. As of the mid-1990s the wave is still a ripple, but it's growing quickly. The U.S. market for desktop videoconferencing systems and services increased 81 percent between 1991 and 1995, says InfoWorld Publishing (as quoted by Patricia Galagan in *Training & Development*'s February 1996 issue). And in *Training* magazine's "Industry Report" survey (October 1995), 43 percent of responding firms said they train employees through videoconferencing, teleconferencing, or distance learning via computer.

In today's business environment, distance learning for various kinds of training and education makes sense for a lot of companies. Distance learning is nothing more than learning that takes place at a site that's remote from where the instruction originates. It encompasses the latest high-tech tools, including electronic mail and interactive teleconferencing via satellite. It also includes such low-tech options as plain old correspondence courses conducted by "snail mail." However, that's not the kind of instruction that is causing a surge in the popularity of distance learning. Various business trends make distance learning sensible, but it's the technological advances that make it viable.

Why does distance learning make sense?

- *Organizations are "going virtual."* They have international sales offices, plants around the world, and multiple locations throughout the country. In metropolitan areas they're cutting traffic, pollution, and commuting time by setting up suburban satellite offices to allow employees to work at sites close to their homes.

- *Organizations are cutting costs.* Everyone is under pressure to do more with less. That includes training more people with less time and fewer resources. Used appropriately, distance learning is quick and inexpensive.

In fact if you need to train a lot of people, distance learning can be extraordinarily cost-effective. Most organizations pay for traditional classroom training on a per-trainee basis, spending at least $100 per person, per day. But distance learning is priced by the program, not the participant. If a satellite program costs $500, an organization that has more than five employees to train can come out ahead by choosing that option. Of course the organization needs to be equipped with a satellite dish or have access to a viewing site. Many universities and community colleges offer access for a fee; even some high schools now have their own satellite dishes!

Distance learning isn't the best solution for every training problem, but it can work well for meeting learning objectives that have to do with conveying information or influencing beliefs. For example, a teleconference might be an effective way of bringing employees of a decentralized firm up to speed on a new corporate sexual-harassment policy. Distance learning is not as effective for training that will require participants to practice a new skill. Even via interactive television, an instructor would be hard-pressed to observe the performance of mechanics at four different plants as they simultaneously try a new welding technique.

The challenge for training and development specialists is to know enough about the technology to make intelligent choices from the options that are available.

MEASURING LEARNING

Considerable attention is now being paid to alternative forms of assessing learning. Why do we perceive a paradigm shift that is moving away from traditional, multiple-choice, standardized achievement tests to alternative forms of assessment? Why do we need a variety of strategies for tracking adult learner performance over time? Why is there renewed interest in finding more systematic ways of looking for connections between what we *do* in training and development and what *changes* occur in employee performance on the job?

THE OUTCOMES-BASED PARADIGM SHIFT

Granted "paradigm" is an increasingly trendy word, but it does capture the dramatic shift that is occurring in how we think about training and development. Paradigms are rules and regulations, stated and unstated assumptions, models and standard procedures that shape our view of the world or our understanding of the ways things are and work.

Paradigms shift when they no longer help us solve problems or explain powerful, fundamental, and emerging changes in our understandings, assumptions, and values. Such a shift is occurring in how trainers view teaching, learning, and assessment. We are beginning to question the accuracy of standardized tests in assessing outcomes important to a training or instructional program. We have gotten too comfortable with designing training and instruction to match the format of multiple-choice testing items; thus there tends to be overemphasis on drill and practice in discrete skills. This is problematic. The concept of learning as the accumulation of bits of knowledge is outmoded. Current models of learning based on cognitive psychology demonstrate that understanding is increased when learners construct their own knowledge and develop cognitive maps of interconnections among concepts and facts.

To engage learners in the kinds of critical thinking that adults will need in the twenty-first century, we will have to shift to a paradigm that focuses on practice in solving real problems and comprehending complex tasks. The establishment of TQM, ISO 9000, business process reengineering, teams, and other modern management systems requires new forms of assessment for outcomes-based training.

What knowledge, skills, and job orientations will adult learners need in order to be prepared to live in the more competitive twenty-first century? The next century will be characterized by an information society, global economic interdependence, cultural pluralism, rapidly expanding technologies, and decentralized social structures. Such a society will be based on knowledge and the ability to put it to work to create, invent, and solve problems.

The emphasis for most workers to possess "basic skills," which characterized educational preparation during the twentieth century, is no longer viable. Instead capacities once demanded of only the top 20 percent of America's society will soon be required of the masses: to think critically and creatively, to solve problems, to exercise judgment, and to learn new skills and knowledge throughout a lifetime.

What Are We Learning About Assessment? This outcomes-based paradigm shift is also shaping how we view assessment. For decades we assumed that assessment was an end in itself. Now we assume that assessment is a vehicle for learning improvement. An outcomes-based view of assessment begins with a vision of the kinds of learning we most value. These values or outcomes drive not only what we choose to assess but also how we do so.

What adult learners bring to the table is not that important. What has become crucial to business is what adult learners can be taught to do with new learning. Therefore, outcomes-based assessment requires a more diverse array of methods that measure actual learner performance over time to reveal change, growth, and increasing degrees of knowledge integration. In other words, our earlier assumptions about assessment as "one-shot" are giving way to an understanding that learning improvement is best facilitated when assessment entails a linked series of activities undertaken over time.

Outcomes-based assessment implies that we design and organize everything we do in training and education around the intended learning demonstration we want to see at the end. We base things on the outcomes so that the outcome will eventually occur for everyone. What might an outcomes-based assessment mean for a management development training program?

We start with the program by identifying what is valued. The management development program might desire four general outcomes for participants: problem solving, analytic capabilities, value judgments, and decision-making skills. Participants do not take a multiple-choice content knowledge test under an outcomes-based paradigm. This test would only measure what discrete facts a person recalled from the training course. Instead participants might be asked to work at an authentic task that will reveal their depth of understanding through applying the management course's new information.

For example, participants might be asked to select an action, taken by an influential person in the company, that had important consequences for that company. They are asked to determine the characteristics of the decision that had to be identified by this person before such an action was taken. What dilemmas did the person face? What alternative choices were available to this person when the decision was made? What criteria was the person likely to have applied in making the decision? What were the possible trade-offs in selecting one alternative over another? What were the risks, the rewards, and the consequences? How might these have been measured? Without benefit of hindsight, would you have made the same decision? Why or why not?

Such an outcomes-based task enables assessment of several indicators of good problem solving:

1. clear definition of a decision question
2. clear articulation of alternatives
3. appropriateness of alternatives
4. clear identification of criteria on which the alternatives were assessed
5. value judgment of the importance of the identified criteria to the overall decision
6. assessment of the extent to which each alternative included or matched up with each of the identified criteria
7. commitment to a final selection among the alternatives
8. adequacy of the final selection to the initial dilemma

Criterion-based assessments and authentic tasks focus on what adult learners can eventually learn to do well, rather than on how well they do the first time they encounter something. Authentic tasks address the outcomes we value and simulate challenges facing an individual on the job. We will explore these specific notions of assessment in the sections that follow.

What Norm-Referenced or Standardized Testing Can and Cannot Tell Us. What norm-referenced or standardized testing tells us is what learners know in general. If we look at a standardized reading test, for example, and focus on all learners with high scores and all learners with low scores, it is likely that more reading difficulties will exist among learners with low scores. Of what use is this kind of information? Standardized tests enable us to get a global picture. In general, are sixth graders learning reading at the sixth grade level? In general, are college algebra students learning college algebra?

However, what standardized testing does not tell us, nor is it meant to tell us, are nuances of performance that characterize the full range of a learner's skill, ability, and learning style. The fact that a reader scores well on a standardized test does not mean that we can say with confidence that the person is a wonderful reader and always will be in all circumstances.

Furthermore, traditional tests are arbitrarily timed, superficial in the content they test, and given only once or twice. They leave us with no way of gauging a learner's ability to make progress over time. So we must ask whether standardized tests provide sufficient information to allow intelligent instructional and program decision making. For example, what does it mean if a learner ranks in the eightieth percentile on a reading test? We may say that person has performed better than 80 percent of the others who took the same test. This sounds impressive. However, a difference in performance on one test item can significantly raise or lower an individual's percentile ranking.

In addition, reading passages in traditional tests are generally shorter and less complex than the texts that learners encounter in daily work. Standardized reading tests use a small number of item types to avoid confusing test takers with frequent changes in format. This is problematic for there is considerable evidence that individuals "may appear to know a concept or skill when it is measured in one format but not know it if measured in another way." Given this, how much confidence do we want to place in standardized test scores for program and personnel decision making?

Do standardized tests have value? Yes, they do. The most immediate value for pre- and poststandardized tests is as an indicator of a learner's initial, general knowledge base. However, as noted in our discussion of the nature of standardized norm-referenced tests, standardized tests are not generally aligned with training and development curricula. Thus, it is important to examine the match between competencies measured on a standardized test and the curriculum of the training or instructional program. It is also important never to assume that test scores are infallible or to use a single test to make an important decision about an individual or a program.

If the primary purpose of assessment is to guide instructional decision making and to provide feedback to learners, then standardized norm-referenced testing falls short of this purpose. More can be accomplished with a combination of methods that include, but are not limited to, standardized measures. Pre- and poststandardized tests, when supplemented by criterion-referenced tests or alternative assessments, such as authentic tasks or curriculum-based measurements, can provide indicators of changes in a learner's knowledge base associated with a training or instructional program. In the following paragraphs we will discuss such alternatives to standardized testing.

Criterion-Referenced Testing. Criterion-referenced tests are tests of specific skills that are scored with reference to examples of poor, fair, good, and excellent performance of those skills. Unlike norm-referenced or standardized tests, which compare any given student's performance in general with that of other test takers, criterion-referenced testing is interpreted in terms of performance criteria that can be more closely aligned with the content and conduct of specific training or instruction. Criterion-referenced tests tell us about a learner's level of proficiency in or mastery of some skill or set of skills. Learners are not compared with others, as in norm-referenced testing, but with a standard of mastery called a *criterion.*

Criterion-referenced testing helps us decide whether a learner needs more or less work on a specific skill or set of skills. It says nothing of the learner's place or rank compared with other learn-ers. Hence, this kind of test provides constantly updated infor-mation about a learner's attained capabilities within a particular program of instruction or training. This information is far more useful in making ongoing training or instructional decisions. Cri-terion-referenced testing enables deficiencies to be precisely diag-nosed and training or instruction to be targeted at addressing those deficiencies.

Criterion-referenced tests must be very specific if they are to yield information about individual skills. Such specificity is useful for enabling teachers and trainers to be relatively certain that learners have mastered or failed to master the skill in question. The disadvantage is that a number of criterion-referenced tests are needed to make decisions about multiple skills.

Criterion-referenced tests require clear and measurable instruc-tional or training objectives. A complete instructional or training objective includes: (1) an observable behavior, (2) any special con-dition under which the behavior must be displayed, and (3) a per-formance level considered sufficient to demonstrate mastery. An example of a complete instructional objective for an adult basic-skills mathematics program might be, "Given a calculator, the learner will multiply two-digit numbers, correct to the nearest whole number, with a 90 percent level of accuracy." An example of a complete instructional objective for a secretarial writing pro-gram might be, "Given a dictionary, the learner will correct spell-ing errors in a sample letter of inquiry with a 95 percent accuracy level."

Where criterion-referenced assessment is used, pre- and post-measurement of the skills that are critical to optimal performance is the only concrete way of assessing whether instructional or training programs are making a difference. It is also important for learners to be able to track their own progress. In both program evaluation and learner feedback, the difficulty is always in finding a systematic way to examine key indicators that are valued in optimal performance.

Curriculum-Based Measurement (CBM). Because norm-referenced tests, and sometimes criterion-referenced measures, are intended for broad use, there is still considerable concern over the mismatch between content of such tests and the content of training or instructional programs. It is important to note, however, that standardized tests make no pretense of fitting training or instructional curricula precisely. What kinds of assessment might have a better fit in this respect?

Curriculum-based measurements (CBMs) are repeated measurements of an adult learner's performance on a single global task across time. They offer multiple assessments of adult learner progress toward a long-term course goal specific to mastering a task. CBMs use the specific curriculum provided in a training or instructional setting as the basis for tracking the adult learner's performance on specific desired outcomes. For example, at the beginning of a train-the-trainer program, the adult learner is given a set of questions pertaining to the personal attributes of a good trainer. Using the provided CBM rating scale, they determine their personal understanding of principles critical to the train-the-trainer learning process. At the end of the train-the-trainer course, the adult learner again is assessed using this same CBM. Of critical importance is how well the rating scale tracks postprogram changes in the degree of individual understanding of train-the-trainer "best training practices."

It is important in CBMs that learners review their performance before each assessment. The goal line, for example, helps learners to monitor their own progress. In addition, progress toward the estimated goal helps instructors make decisions about modifying instruction, changing the level of reading passages, or modifying the goal line.

A CBM that could be applied to a management development program would be to monitor and assess effective communication within a work team by using a two-minute reading/response passage for each participant. This reading passage might be used on a weekly basis and the accuracy of responses calculated.

Participants' progress (accuracy of responses) is graphed. An optimal performance, or goal line, might be determined by using the average of participants' performances on two baseline scenarios and adding a percentage of accurate responses to the score as a target for improvement. It is again important in CBMs that learners review their performance before each assessment to monitor their own progress.

Several factors must be taken into consideration when designing CBMs:

1. Select tasks that will represent those the adult learner is expected to perform in class/training sessions. Such tasks can be taken directly from sample curriculum materials being used.

2. Remember that CBMs are timed. Keep the measurement short, for example, one to five minutes. The purpose of the CBM is to track learner performance in multiple tasks over time.

3. CBMs are most useful when they are given frequently, for example, every other day, or twice a week, depending upon the length of the class/training session. Useful measurement occurs when the measurement task looks and functions like any other class/training session task. In other words learners should not feel like they are taking a test.

4. CBMs can be normed. Give the same measurement to a sample of five to ten learners identified by the supervisor/ employer as average peers of the learner. Or, if the trainer/ employer wants to compare the learner's performance against optimally desired performance, the five to ten learn-

ers might be selected from among top-rated on-the-job performers. The performance of this sample of five to ten
average or optimal learners sets the baseline for comparison
of the individual learner's performance against the norm.
5. The most effective way to represent learner growth is graph-
ically. Norm performance, or goal-related performance, and
the learner's actual performance can be charted on a line
graph.

Why bother with better assessments? Unfortunately there is a
shocking lack of systematic assessment and applied research to
enrich our state-of-the-art and best-practice knowledge about
workforce education. Research and evaluation data tend to be collected in uneven ways. When programs are evaluated, assessment
data are often limited to sketchy descriptions of program components, anecdotal recountings as indicators of effectiveness, questionnaires and surveys of program participants, and incomplete
references to learner performance results. Occasionally standardized test results may be provided, but standardized tests are useful
indicators of general ability only. They are not specific to program
curricula.

Better assessments are built upon three key assumptions. First,
assessment is seen as integral to learning. The one-shot notion of
assessment celebrated in standardized tests does not fit an emerging developmental and constructivist view of knowledge and
understanding. The major purpose of assessment should be to aid
learning. Assessment cannot be conceived as a series of discrete
milestones but as part of a continuous and coherent learning
process.

Second, assessment is linked to outcomes. Learning and understanding go beyond *what* one knows to what one *does* with that
knowledge. Thus it is important that assessments directly relate to
instructional and training objectives. Assessments that reflect specific and explicit criteria for performance, continuous feedback,

and self-assessment are more effective in capturing performance of valued outcomes over time.

Third, abilities must be developed and assessed in multiple modes and contexts. Most abilities and the real-life situations in which they are tested are multidimensional and complex. Assessment should provide learners with repeated opportunities to experience, practice, and assess their performance in varied contexts and at varied levels of mastery.

The more we understand about these alterable constructs associated with learning, the more likely we are to develop training and education programs and assessments that contribute to greater learner success.

TRAINING'S ECONOMIC VALUE ADDED (EVA)

The current trend to measure cost throughout a business means that senior executives are showing increasing interest in determining the economic value added by every department, including training. The bad news is that senior managers tend to see training and education as an ivory tower. As one AMA business roundtable participant noted, "We often feel that (training) managers don't know the business."

Why are so few companies reskilling their employees? A U.S. Labor Department survey (October 1994) of nearly 12,000 businesses found that, as of 1993, fewer than half were offering their workers formal job-skills training essential for improved productivity. Worse yet, fewer than 3 percent were offering training in basic reading, writing, math, or English as a second language.

Equally depressing news came from the National Education Goals Panel describing the fact (October 1994) that only 52 percent of the U.S. adult population scored at level 3 or higher on the prose portion of the National Adult Literacy Survey (NALS) conducted in 1992. Nearly half of all American adults are not able to perform the range of complex literacy tasks considered important for successful U.S. competition in a global economy.

We do not have to look far to see how these results are playing out in daily American life. According to recently released U.S. Census Bureau data (October 1994), the median income of the average American family has declined each year since 1991. This trend persists despite rising levels in employment, productivity, and total national income. Why? Because, reports the *Wall Street Journal* (October 26, 1994), economists believe, "that the most valuable spark to setting median income on an upward trajectory may now lie primarily in long-term costly solutions—particularly retraining workers for high-skill jobs and investing in education." If this trend does not change, how will the middle class still drive the American economic machine? It seems that hard times are ahead for many American businesses.

So why do so few businesses attempt to reeducate their own workers in light of these potential grave economic consequences? There seem to be two major roadblocks:

1. Doubt about the credibility of the providers of skills training and about the results of such training.
2. A lack of understanding concerning the economic value added (return-on-investment) that skills training will give to any business.

Finance managers have also argued that it is not realistic to measure the long-term, qualitative effects of training and educational programs. We beg to differ. Here are several economic-value-added (EVA) measuring systems that trainers can use to calculate your management or skill training programs' return-on-investment.

UTILITY ANALYSIS (ADDED VALUE)

How much is any training program worth? Utility analysis is a hard-data method for determining return-on-investment (ROI) for training by calculating the value of an intervention (i.e., a training program) minus its cost. Economic gain equals the training effect times the monetary value of that effect. This produced the following utility analysis equation:

Where $F = N[(E \times M) - C]$
   F = financial utility
   N = number of people trained
   E = effect of the training on the business
   M = monetary value of the training effect
   C = cost of the training per person

Casio (*Training and Development in Organizations,* Jossey-Bass, 1989) and Godkeivitsch (*Training* magazine, May 1987) both have written clear and detailed descriptions of how to use the utility analysis method over a broad range of training content and methods.

TIME VALUE OF MONEY

The National Planning Association has addressed training ROI in Crawrods and Webley's *Continuing Education and Training of the Workforce* (1992). This is also an added-value approach through calculating the opportunity cost of training. The authors offer a set of economic formulas that compare a company's investment in a specific training program to other potential forms of investment. They give a step-by-step method for a company's financial officer to determine if the training productivity increase will give a greater ROI than investing the company's money in capital improvements and so forth.

PERFORMANCE VALUE

A third method is offered by Swanson and Gradous in *Forecasting Financial Benefits of Human Resource Development* (Jossey-Bass, 1988). They argue that it is better to forecast the potential results than to later evaluate the effect of training. Performance value helps businesses to choose among training program options before investing in any program, rather than waiting to evaluate after the training has been completed.

This forecasting approach forces the business to determine the fiscal value of the operational problems to be addressed by the training program. How will quality, time, costs, and output issues translate into specific quantifiable training results? Swanson and Gradous offer a worksheet to calculate the performance value of a training program.

HOW PRACTICAL?

To accomplish effective ROI, trainers must first receive approval from senior management and their financial people for a specific financial analysis model and an acceptable rate of return. They need to be involved in determining how that return on training that meets a real operational need is calculated and measured. Remember that achieving a good, feasible rate-of-return (profit) in senior management's eyes is what the business is all about. Bringing the training department "on line" as another "revenue center" rather than just another "cost" means you are finally providing the monetary proof that investing in people will be profitable for any business. This holds equally true for either basic skill programs or more traditional management development. Total quality management (TQM) and other quality team efforts are contemporary areas in which ROI for training is gaining widespread interest. Poor quality in products or services costs in terms of the economic value added. High potential training payoffs will only be reached if the specific education programs precisely uncover local TQM operational problems. European Union (EU) members and the Japanese have clearly demonstrated how high productivity gains can be achieved by using training to correct substantial business problems.

When will American senior managers also acknowledge the realities of the modern workplace and place workforce education on the cutting edge of business?

THE REAL BOTTOM-LINE MESSAGE

The immediate return-on-investment practices of American corporations are threatening contemporary workplace innovation. American managers do not equate investment in human capital (through education/training) that has the potential for producing dazzling innovations with capital investment in equipment or buildings. Most U.S. business leaders now believe that it is too costly to train or retrain the American worker.

The chief issue that seems to drive most American boardrooms in this direction is the quarterly financial return. In the short term it seems far cheaper for many companies either to relocate overseas, where they can find the well-educated, technically ready employees they need, or to sell off their technology for a quick profit. Examples abound.

RCA developed the liquid crystal display (LCD) technology and sold its concept to Timex of Japan. Ampex invented magnetic videotape technology only to sell it to Sony. Rockwell sold Sharp its semiconductor patent. Hewlett-Packard designs and builds laserjet printer technology overseas to import back to the United States.

Many other multinational corporations are increasingly falling into the same pattern. On and on this list grows as markets worth at least tens of billions of dollars, capital investment, and human education investment all benefit societies other than our own.

The major long-term economic consequences of this business scenario is that, unless this pattern changes, the United States will develop into a two-tier society of high-wage/high-educated employees versus low-wage/low-educated workers. Left unchecked, this business trend will gradually undermine the American middle class and our consumer-driven economic system. Signs of this change have already begun with the continued wage erosion of middle-class workers who comprise the bulk of U.S. consumers. Who then will be left to buy these products being made overseas? Will U.S. business continue to thrive regardless of these long-term economic shifts? Or will American business be bought off by foreign investors and the United States become another postindustrial nation, such as Great Britain, where Jaguar is owned by Ford and Rover by BMW?

Is the average German, Japanese, or Korean worker more innately intelligent or technically astute than the average American worker? The many case studies of financially successful skill training and educational programs within American companies presented in such books as *Closing the Literacy Gap in American Business* (1991) and *FutureWork: The Revolution Reshaping American Business* (1994) make the authors say they don't think so!

American business needs to learn from its chief foreign competitors that its employees are key resources capable of development. Training professionals need to help their companies adopt a workforce education policy so that any organization may use a proven economic-value-added concept—that human knowledge equals profit.

CHAPTER 7

PROFESSIONAL INFORMATION AND NETWORKING

Everybody pays lip service to the importance of networking, but few people are doing it on a regular basis. In training and development, networking is a good way of making and maintaining contacts—contacts that might be helpful later, when you need information, a job, or a supplier. It's a way of staying current and connected, both in the training field and in the industry your training affects. It's a way to make your name and services known among your peers and potential clients. It also can open up opportunities to contribute to the field in a larger way than your regular job allows.

BUILDING YOUR NETWORK

The best way to make meaningful connections outside your own organization is to put yourself in places where you're likely to run into the kinds of people you want to meet. Sign up for courses or seminars. Go to conferences. Join professional organizations, attend their meetings, and run for office.

Some otherwise savvy businesspeople take advantage of such opportunities only if their employers are footing the bill. That's fine if your department has deep pockets and a hefty professional-development budget for its own staff. But in today's business world, professional development tends to be the joint responsibility of you and your employer. If the boss says there's no money to send you to a dynamite conference, suggest a compromise: You pay all or part of your travel expenses and registration fees, and the boss provides paid time off for you to attend. Most employers will be impressed that you're willing to go the extra mile.

Once you're there, talk to people. Ask questions about what they do and describe your own areas of interest. When someone gives you a business card, jot down a few words on the back to remind yourself of who this person is and, perhaps, what information you promised to send. Remember that networking goes both ways. Think about how you can help—not just about what's in it for you. Then follow up with a phone call or package of information. That follow-up is vital. If you have nothing specific to send—such as an article that you think will be of interest—then just find reasons to keep in touch. A holiday greeting card or a note of congratulations on a new job can keep your name fresh in someone's mind. Many close friendships began as networking relationships between colleagues.

Networking can happen inside your company as well as outside it. If there's a department or field office you might be interested in working with (or for) at some time in the future, drop by or put in a phone call now. Take somebody to lunch and ask questions. Most people will be flattered by your interest.

Networking doesn't have to be face-to-face. Say you're looking for information on how to set up a distance-education course. However, you're on a tight deadline and the next big conference on that issue is six months away. By all means sign up for the conference, but in the meantime you have other options for making contacts. Remember that training organization you joined? Now is when you learn what the membership directory is for. Find other members who have listed themselves as distance-learning professionals and pick up the phone. Identifying yourself as a member of the same professional society—even one with thousands of members—is generally enough of a connection so that people will be happy to answer your questions or recommend suppliers.

New technology provides more state-of-the-art ways of making contacts and keeping in touch. The American Society for Training and Development has an online service that allows subscribers to keep in touch with each other through electronic mail, "real-time" electronic discussions, and forums on various training-related topics. It also provides bibliographic references and full text on a variety of training-related articles, as well as Internet access. Another high-tech option is a training and development *listserv* operated through Pennsylvania State University. A listserv is kind of a virtual, never-ending discussion group. Joining is simple and free. Once you're on the distribution list, you can post messages for all the other members to see, and you'll receive the messages they post, as well. For instance, you post a message to the listserv, saying, "I'm putting together a distance-learning program. Does anyone know where I can get access to a satellite dish in these specific regions around the country?" If your topic sparks people's interest, you could have more responses in a few days than you have time to read.

For information on joining ASTD Online, call ASTD at 703/683–8100. To subscribe to the training and development listserv operated out of Pennsylvania State University, you must already have access to the Internet. Send an e-mail message to listserv @psuvm.psu.edu with SUB TRDEV-L YOUR NAME in the body of the message.

WHY YOU SHOULD JUST DO IT

We've seen that networking is easy, educational, flexible, and helpful. It can even be fun and lead to long-term friendships. Why, then, are so few people doing any meaningful, purposeful networking on a regular basis? The reasons they give tend to fall into several categories:

- "I don't have time to network."
- "I tried networking once. It didn't do any good."

- "I don't need to network. I already have a job."
- "I'm not in a position to network. I don't even have a job!"

There's a simple answer to the first reason: Make time. Stop thinking of developing contacts as a luxury. Think of it as part of your job and part of your long-term career development.

The second reason listed above shows a focus on short-term results and unreasonable expectations. Networking is long term. Don't think that you'll meet a colleague at a seminar today and receive a job offer from that person tomorrow. It happens, but not often. A more likely scenario is that the person you meet at a seminar today is the one who puts you in touch with someone who hires you six years from now. But that will only happen if you attend that seminar and if you follow up with the contacts you make there.

The last two reasons cancel each other out. Some people don't network because they don't need a job. Others don't network because they don't have a job. By now it should be clear that getting a job is not the only point of networking. It's not even the main point. When it does happen, it happens because of a long-term relationship. So don't wait until you're unemployed to start.

What if it's too late for that? You've already lost your job, or you're trying to break into the field and haven't found that first job. Sometimes a newcomer to a field will say, "I couldn't possibly go to that society's program! Everyone there will be an expert in the field. I'm just a beginner. They'll think I have no business being there." In most fields that fear is unfounded. The kind of people who get involved in their professional organizations tend to be the kind of people who want to help their profession. And part of the profession is helping newcomers to it. In training and development that's doubly true. People in training and development tend to believe in, well, professional development. It's an occupational hazard. Don't expect a real career-counseling session for free. However, most people are happy to answer a few questions or give you the name of someone else who can help.

WHERE TO NETWORK

Training and development professionals belong to a wide variety of professional organizations. Such groups offer publications, networking opportunities, information on the field, professional support, conferences, and seminars. Some services are only for members. Others are available to anyone.

Some groups, such as the American Society for Training and Development, are comprehensive in scope. Others cover particular industries (such as the American Society for Healthcare Education and Training) or certain kinds of learning vehicles (such as the United States Distance Learning Association).

ORGANIZATIONS THAT CAN HELP

Here's a list of some of the organizations you might try, either for membership or other kinds of information and support:

Adult Education Association
810 Eighteenth Street NW
Washington, DC 20006

American Association for Adult and Continuing Education
1200 Nineteenth Street NW
Suite 300
Washington, DC 20036

American Management Association
135 West Fiftieth Street
New York, NY 10020

American Society for Healthcare Education and Training
840 North Lake Shore Drive
Chicago, IL 60611

American Society for Training and Development
1640 King Street, Box 1443
Alexandria, VA 22313–2043

American Vocational Association
1410 King Street
Alexandria, VA 22314

Association for Experiential Education
    University of Colorado
    Box 249
    Boulder, CO 80309

Association for Quality and Participation
    801-B West Eighth Street
    Suite 501
    Cincinnati, OH 45203–1607

Commission on Adult Basic Education
    Auburn University
    Auburn, AL 36830

Industrial Relations Research Association
    University of Wisconsin
    7226 Social Science Building
    1180 Observatory Drive
    Madison, WI 53706

International Personnel Management Association
    1617 Duke Street
    Alexandria, VA 22314

International Society for Performance Improvement
    1126 Sixteenth Street NW
    Suite 102
    Washington, DC 20036

Organizational Behavior Teaching Society
    Bureau of Business Research and Services
    Box U-41 Br
    Storrs, CT 06268

Society for Applied Learning Technology
    50 Culpeper Street
    Warrenton, VA 22186

Society for Human Resource Management
    606 North Washington Street
    Alexandria, VA 22314

United States Distance Learning Association
    Box 5129
    San Ramon, CA 94583

PUBLICATIONS TO LOOK INTO

The following periodicals can be helpful to people who are entering the field of training, workplace education, and organization development. Savvy training specialists also keep up with general business news through periodicals such as the *Wall Street Journal, Business Week,* and industry-specific journals.

Adult Education
Adult Education Association
810 Eighteenth Street NW
Washington, DC 20006

Adult Literacy and Basic Education
Commission on Adult Basic Education
Auburn University
Auburn, AL 36830

American Education Quarterly: A Journal of Research and Theory
American Association for Adult and Continuing Education
1200 Nineteenth Street NW
Suite 300
Washington, DC 20036

ASTD Trainer's Toolkits
American Society for Training and Development
1640 King Street
Box 1443
Alexandria, VA 22313–2043

Career Planning and Adult Development Journal
Career Planning and Adult Development Network
4965 Sierra Road
San Jose, CA 95132

Education Technology: The Magazine for Managers of Change in Education
Educational Technology Publications
700 Palisades Avenue
Englewood Cliffs, NJ 07632

Educational Technology Systems
 Society for Applied Learning Technology
 50 Culpeper Street
 Warrenton, VA 22186

Exchange: The Organizational Behavior Teaching Journal
 Organizational Behavior Teaching Society
 Bureau of Business Research and Services
 Box U-41 Br
 Storrs, CT 06268

Group and Organization Management: An International Journal
 Sage Publications
 2455 Teller Road
 Thousand Oaks, CA 91320

Group and Organization Studies: The International Journal for
    Group Facilitators
 University Associates
 Box 26240
 San Diego, CA 92126

HRMagazine
 Society for Human Resource Management
 606 North Washington Street
 Alexandria, VA 22314

Human Performance
 Lawrence Erlbaum Associates
 365 Broadway
 Hillsdale, NJ 07642

Human Resource Development Quarterly
 University of Minnesota
 Training and Development Research Center
 1954 Buford Avenue
 St. Paul, MN 55108

Industrial and Commercial Training
 MCB University Press
 62 Toller Lane, Bradford
 West Yorkshire, England BD8 9BY

Info-Line
   American Society for Training and Development
   1640 King Street
   Box 1443
   Alexandria, VA 22313–2043

The Journal for Quality and Participation
   Association for Quality and Participation
   801-B West Eighth Street
   Suite 501
   Cincinnati, OH 45203–1607

Journal of European Industrial Training
   MCB University Press
   62 Toller Lane, Bradford
   West Yorkshire, England BD8 9BY

Journal of Management Development
   MCB University Press
   62 Toller Lane, Bradford
   West Yorkshire, England BD8 9BY

Lifelong Learning: The Adult Years
   Adult Education Association
   810 Eighteenth Street NW
   Washington, DC 20006

Technical & Skills Training
   American Society for Training and Development
   1640 King Street
   Box 1443
   Alexandria, VA 22313–2043

Training & Development
   American Society for Training and Development
   1640 King Street
   Box 1443
   Alexandria, VA 22313–2043

Training magazine
   Lakewood Publications
   731 Hennepin Avenue
   Minneapolis, MN 55403

CHAPTER 8

THE FUTURE AT "CORPORATE U."

A RENAISSANCE FOR LEARNING
IN AMERICAN BUSINESS

The "corporate university," the "learning organization," "life-long employee learning," and "knowledge-creating companies," are now part of the American business culture bandwagon that recognizes the links between learning and continuous improvement. What is its impact on companies large or small? How did this movement come into being? Where is it going?

The idea of a corporate university brings to mind for many their past college days. For contemporary American business the word *university* is an effort to collectively organize the delivery of information and learning to any employee. The current torrent of books and articles represents a rediscovery, or renaissance, as business grapples with the knowledge explosion felt throughout contemporary society.

A BRIEF HISTORY OF THE CORPORATE UNIVERSITY

This has happened before. Between 1895 and 1920 businesses in the United States upheld general learning for all Americans by supporting the nationwide effort that established universal, tax-supported, public education. A highly literate workforce was seen as an asset in most workplaces to support assembly-line manufacturing based on Frederick Taylor's principles of scientific management.

During World War I (1914–1918) business took education a step further into the workplace by adopting Charles R. Allen's four-step method (show, tell, do, and check) as the standard method for on-the-job training (OJT) that supported burgeoning assembly-line war industries.

World War II (1941–1945) sparked an expansion of workplace education. Job instructor training (JIT) was designed as a train-the-trainer system for first-line and second-line supervisors to support the vast expansion of assembly-line production in the U.S. defense industry. More than two million employees received corporate training in JIT, job methods, and human relations.

For the first time in American history, the Engineering, Science and Management War Training program (ESMWT), established during World War II, and the GI Bill, exposed millions of adults to college courses on almost every aspect of management, technology, psychology, and education. The idea of the corporate university was not far behind for by the mid-1950s, these newly educated managers formalized the use of in-house training and education programs. These early corporate universities were built around the concepts of management behavior and managing human resource development (HRD).

By the mid-1980s the Carnegie Foundation reported that business had invested more than $40 billion in the employee education efforts, reaching almost eight million employees annually. This represented a wide range of in-house education programs, seminars, and institutes teaching everything from computer skills and management techniques to sales and customer service. In addition there was a growing emphasis on basic skills training.

As the idea of offering a diversity of educational programs to a broad array of employees took hold, American companies began to formally build corporate university facilities. The Xerox Center in Virginia, the RCA Campus in New Jersey, the Holiday Inn University in Mississippi, and the Motorola, Arthur Andersen, and McDonald's facilities in Illinois, began to look very much like traditional college campuses with classrooms, dormitories, and recreational facilities. The growth of these facilities, and their relative impact on overall American business culture, began to establish the idea that employee education meant something far more than just narrow training. By 1988 eight corporations purported to offer about twenty college-level degree programs! The U.S. corporate university existed both as a broad educational concept and as an accredited degree-granting institution.

CURRENT REALITY

Today corporate universities of all types and sizes operate throughout the country, from Procter & Gamble College to IRS University. Yet all share a common mission: to transform the department, corporation, agency, or institution into a learning organization.

Just visualizing this concept of learning in a business environment is an enormous problem. Calvert, Mobley, and Marshall provide a useful blueprint for putting the theory of a learning organization—and corporate university—into practice (see Figure 8.1).

Wabash National in Lafayette, Indiana, shows how the concept works in real life. In 1985, working from a card table and three folding chairs in a downtown Lafayette, Indiana, office, Donald J. Ehrlich began Wabash National to build truck trailers. This company's managers, besides calling suppliers whom they already knew for orders, also called on Purdue University's management department for training. "The philosophy was that the people at Wabash were either going to make it or break it," says Chuck

Figure 8.1.   Blueprint for a Learning Organization

WHAT DOES A LEARNING ORGANIZATION LEARN?

What do learning organizations learn that other organizations do not? Learning organizations learn:

§ to use learning to reach their goals

§ to help people value the effects of their learning on their organizations

§ to avoid making the same mistakes again (and again)

§ to share information in ways that prompt appropriate action

§ to link individual performance with organizational performance

§ to tie reward to key measures of performance

§ to take in a lot of environmental information at all times

§ to create structures and procedures that support the learning process

§ to foster ongoing and orderly dialogues

§ to make it safe for people to share openly and take risks

WHAT DOES A LEARNING ORGANIZATION LOOK LIKE?

A learning organization:

§ learns collaboratively, openly, and across boundaries

§ values *how* it learns as well as *what* it learns

§ invests in staying ahead of the learning curve in its industry

§ gains a competitive edge by learning faster and smarter than competitors

§ turns data into useful knowledge quickly and at the right time and place

§ enables every employee to feel that every experience provides him or her a chance to learn something

potentially useful, even if only leveraging future learning

§ exhibits little fear and defensiveness; rewards and learns from what goes wrong ("failure" learning) and right ("success" learning)

§ takes risks but avoids jeopardizing basic security of the organization

§ invests in experimental and seemingly tangential learning

§ supports people and teams who want to pursue action-learning projects

§ depoliticizes learning by not penalizing individuals or groups for sharing information and conclusions

HOW DOES A LEARNING ORGANIZATION EVOLVE?

What are the first steps to becoming a learning organization? A budding learning organization can begin by:

§ questioning current assumptions about learning

§ getting an outside perspective

§ tying the goal of becoming a learning organization to its organizational vision

§ finding or creating a champion in top management

§ looking for the "pain" in the organization—the place where more effective learning could help

§ articulating learning-organization ideas plainly

§ rewarding group as well as individual learning success and failure

§ finding an external enemy to spur greater cooperative learning

§ finding ways to collaborate internally, unhampered by boundaries

Adapted from Calvert, Mobley, and Marshall. "Grasping the Learning Organization." *Training & Development*, June 1994.

Fisk, vice president of human relations in a front page story from the *Wall Street Journal* (September 7, 1995).

They began classes for workers who wanted to become welders and for recent immigrants who wanted to learn English. A worker complained to Ehrlich that he was wasting his profit-sharing (part of the company's participatory motivational culture) on parking lot improvements. Ehrlich responded by adding a course in business basics. Now everyone can learn the difference between a capitalized expense (paving parking lots) and an operating expense (a load of parts). This is part of a series of classes in business economics, statistical process control, the just-in-time inventory system, and team building.

All workers and managers have the opportunity to improve their skills (to comprehend the message), receive training in basic business systems, and then be educated in the problem-solving, decision-making, team-building process. Wabash depends on its workers to learn how a company makes a profit and how rapid growth and constant change will keep them profitable. Ehrlich says at Wabash, "We're trying to get workers to think about building trailers."

Over the last two years workers have participated in 164 practical teams such as the air-brake stroke and free-play adjustment team. These groups have saved the company hundreds of thousands of dollars through practical, thoughtful production innovations.

Does Wabash support a corporate university? At Wabash, Jerry Ehrlich says, "three Einsteins would be no match" for a factory full of workers attending classes and contributing ideas. This is the essence of the learning organization/corporate university concept.

American business is at the end of an era of only managers controlling people, information, and ideas. Victor Hugo was right: "Nothing in the world is as powerful as an idea whose time has come." We have entered the era of the corporate university concept for every organization large or small.

A WATERSHED ERA

The corporate university philosophy will become more pervasive throughout U.S. businesses with each passing year. Some say the next step will be a "virtual university," where workers cobble together learning from courses offered through in-house training, private seminars, and educational institutions. Distance learning, or "education on tap," cannot satisfy every employee educational need. However, the mixed use of high-performance, computer-assisted learning, and face-to-face instruction will continue to steadily grow throughout the corporate classroom, putting both large and small business players on a far more equal information/ learning footing.

Enter the "virtual training organization" (VTO). This "learning university" approach offers a varied menu of learning methods, including interactive computer technology, self-directed learning tools, and customized packages of print materials. The VTO university may feature self-paced workbooks, self-study courses, CD-ROM instructional packages, and a formal mentoring-coaching process.

In Silicon Valley, National Semiconductor's University is both global and virtual. It networks various academic institutions, business learners, training suppliers, and customers on three continents. This university's goal is to spread a learning vision and philosophy that develops the intellectual capital for future change.

U.S. business has passed from an era of large corporate bureaucracies to a new period where even bigger businesses are trying to organize around smaller work units. Technical invention will continue to accelerate. Yet increasing value will be placed on fostering personal creativity and innovation. The learning job of any business, whether a multinational corporation, a midsized business of 500 people, or a small family proprietor, is to develop its human capital by maturing it through a lifelong learning process. This is the ultimate goal of the corporate university philosophy and the ultimate challenge for future training and development professionals.

BIBLIOGRAPHY

BOOKS

Allen, Edith., editor. *ASTD Trainer's Toolkit: Job Descriptions in HRD.* Alexandria, VA: ASTD, 1990.

Bellman, Geoffrey. *The Consultant's Calling.* San Francisco: Jossey-Bass, 1990.

Brinkerhoff, Robert O. and Stephen J. Gill. *The Learning Alliance: Systems Thinking in Human Resource Development.* San Francisco: Jossey-Bass, 1994.

Caffarella, Rosemary S. *Planning Programs for Adult Learners.* San Francisco, Jossey-Bass, 1994.

Carnevale, Anthony P., Leila J. Gainer, and J. Villet. *Training in America: The Organization and Strategic Role of Training.* San Francisco: Jossey-Bass, 1990.

Carnevale, Anthony P., Leila J. Gainer, and Eric Schulz. *Training the Technical Work Force.* Alexandria, VA: ASTD and Jossey-Bass, 1990.

Carnevale, Anthony P., Leila J. Gainer, and Ann S. Meltzer. *Workplace Basics: The Essential Skills Employers Want.* Alexandria, VA: ASTD and Jossey-Bass, 1990.

Chang, Richard. *An Introduction to Human Resource Development Careers,* 3d edition. Alexandria, VA: ASTD, 1990.

Craig, Robert L., editor. *Training and Development Handbook: A Guide to Human Resource Development,* 3d edition. New York: McGraw-Hill, 1987.

Gordon, Edward E., Ronald R. Morgan, and Judith A. Ponticell. *Closing the Literacy Gap in American Business: A Guide for Trainers and Human Resource Specialists.* Glenview, IL: Quorum, 1991.

Gordon, Edward E., Ronald R. Morgan, and Judith A. Ponticell. *FutureWork: The Revolution Reshaping American Business.* Glenview, IL: Praeger, 1994.

Gutteridge, Thomas, Zandy Leibowitz, and Jane Shore. *Organizational Career Development: Benchmarks for Building a World-Class Workforce.* Alexandria, VA: ASTD and Jossey-Bass, 1993.

Helfand, David P. *Career Change: Everything You Need to Know to Meet New Challenges and Take Control of Your Career.* Lincolnwood, IL: VGM Career Horizons, 1995.

143

Kelly, Leslie, editor. *The ASTD Technical and Skills Training Handbook.* Alexandria, VA: ASTD and McGraw-Hill, 1995.

Malouf, Doug. *How to Create and Deliver a Dynamic Presentation.* Alexandria, VA: ASTD, 1993.

Marquardt, Michael J. and Dean W. Engel. *Global Human Resource Development.* Englewood Cliffs, NJ: Prentice-Hall, 1993.

McLagan, Patricia. *Models for HRD Practice.* Alexandria, VA: ASTD, 1989.

Meister, Jeanne C. *Corporate Quality Universities: Lessons in Building a World-Class Work Force.* Alexandria, VA: ASTD and Irwin Professional Publishing, 1993.

Occupational Outlook Handbook 1994–1995. U.S. Department of Labor, 1994.

Pace, R. Wayne, Phillip C. Smith, and Gordon E. Mills. *Human Resource Development: The Field.* Englewood Cliffs, NJ: Prentice-Hall, 1991.

Pfeiffer, J. William, editor. *The 1996 Annual: Volume I Training.* San Diego: Pfeiffer & Co, 1996.

Piskurich, George M., editor. *The ASTD Handbook of Instructional Technology.* Alexandria, VA: ASTD and McGraw-Hill, 1992.

Pont, Tony. *Developing Effective Training Skills.* McGraw-Hill Book Company-Europe, 1991.

Powers, Bob. *Instructor Excellence: Mastering the Delivery of Training.* San Francisco: Jossey-Bass, 1992.

Reynolds, Angus. *The Trainer's Dictionary: HRD Terms, Abbreviations, and Acronyms.* Amherst, MA: HRD Press, 1993.

Rothwell, William J. and Henry J. Sredl. *The ASTD Reference Guide to Professional Human Resource Development Roles and Competencies,* 2d edition. Volumes 1 and 2. Amherst, MA: HRD Press, 1992.

Senge, Peter M. *The Fifth Discipline: The Art and Practice of the Learning Organization.* New York: Doubleday, 1990.

Stump, Robert. *Your Career in Human Resource Development: A Guide to Information and Decision Making,* 2d edition. Alexandria, VA: ASTD, 1990.

Svenson, Raynold A. and Monica J. Rinderer. *The Training and Development Strategic Plan Workbook.* Englewood Cliffs, NJ: Prentice-Hall, 1992.

Tracey, William R. *The Human Resources Glossary.* AMACOM, 1991.

Traynor, William J. and J. Steven McKenzie. *Opportunities in Human Resource Management Careers.* Lincolnwood, IL: VGM Career Horizons, 1994.

Worker Training: Competing in the New International Economy. A report prepared by the U.S. Congress Office of Technology Assessment, U.S. Government Printing Office, 1990.

JOURNAL AND MAGAZINE ARTICLES

"Are You Overworked?" (in "FaxForum Results"). *Training & Development,* June 1993.

Argyris, Chris. "The Future of Workplace Learning and Performance." *Training & Development,* May 1994.

Blake, Robert R. "Memories of HRD." *Training & Development,* March 1995.

Blitzer, Roy J. "Guiding People into the Profession." *Training & Development,* December 1988.

Carnevale, Anthony P. "Learning: The Critical Technology." *Training & Development,* February 1992.

Carnevale, Ellen S. "On Target: This Is Your Career." *Technical & Skills Training,* May/June 1993.

Clements, Christine, Richard J. Wagner, and Christopher C. Roland. "The Ins and Outs of Experiential Training." *Training & Development,* February 1995.

Cohen, Stephen L. "The Challenge of Training in the Nineties." *Training & Development,* July 1991.

Corrigan, Marilyn and Sally Sparhawk. "Becoming an Outside Consultant." *Info-Line,* March 1994.

Filipczak, Bob. "The Training Manager in the Nineties." *Training,* June 1994.

Galagan, Patricia A. "Reinventing the Profession." *Training & Development,* December 1994.

Galagan, Patricia A. "Signs of the Times." *Training & Development,* February 1996.

Geber, Beverly. "Re-engineering the Training Department." *Training,* May 1994.

Gill, Stephen J. "Shifting Gears for High Performance." *Training & Development,* May 1995.

Hequet, Marc. "Not Paid Enough? You're Not Alone." *Training,* November 1995.

"How Did You Get Your Start in Training?" (in "FaxForum Results"). *Training & Development,* March 1995.

Hunter, Hal. "Distance Learning and the Feds" (in "The Opposite Sector"). *Training & Development,* May 1995.

Kirk, James J. "Exploring How HRD Managers Differ from Other Managers." *Human Resource Development Quarterly,* winter 1991.

Koonce, Richard. "Becoming Your Own Career Coach." *Training & Development,* January 1995.

Leach, James A. "Characteristics of Excellent Trainers: A Psychological and Interpersonal Profile." *Performance Improvement Quarterly* 4, no. 3 (1991).

Marquardt, Michael J. and Dean W. Engel. "HRD Competencies for a Shrinking World." *Training & Development,* May 1993.

McIntosh, Stephen S. "Envisioning the Virtual Training Organization." *Training & Development,* May 1995.

McLagan, Pat. "Creating the Future of HRD." *Training & Development,* January 1996.

"1995 Industry Report: A Statistical Picture of Employee Training in America." *Training,* October 1995.

Orlin, Jay M. "The Mix That Makes a Good Instructional Designer." *Technical & Skills Training,* October 1992.

"The Past, Present, and Future of Workplace Learning." *Training & Development,* May 1994.

Petrini, Catherine M. "Getting a Foot in the Door" (in "Four by Four"). *Training & Development,* April 1989.

Petrini, Catherine M. "Putting a Price on Your Head" (in "Four by Four"). *Training & Development,* July 1990.

"Quality Training." *Technical & Skills Training,* November/December 1991.

Regalbuto, Gloria. "Recovery from Occupational Schizophrenia." *Training & Development,* May 1991.

Rhinesmith, Stephen H. "Open the Door to a Global Mindset." *Training & Development,* May 1995.

Thomas, Rebecca. "Trainers at the Top of the Earnings Heap" (in "In Practice"). *Training & Development,* May 1995.

"Trainers Network on the Net." *Training & Development,* August 1994.

"What Are Training Consultants Worth?" (in "FaxForum Results"). *Training & Development,* August 1994.

"What's Your Dream Job?" (in "FaxForum Results"). *Training & Development,* December 1994.